D0995896

CHESHIRE RAILWAYS

Robin Jones

THE AGE OF STEAM

COUNTRYSIDE BOOKS
NEWBURY BERKSHIRE

First published 2011
© Robin Jones 2011

COUNTRYSIDE BOOKS
3 Catherine Road
Newbury, Berkshire

To view our complete range of books,
please visit us at
www.countrysidebooks.co.uk

ISBN 978 1 84674 155 5

To Ross, Vicky and Jenny

*And with special thanks to
the National Railway Museum in York*

Designed by Peter Davies, Nautilus Design
Produced through MRM Associates Ltd., Reading
Typeset by CJWT Solutions, St Helens
Printed by Information Press, Oxford

Contents

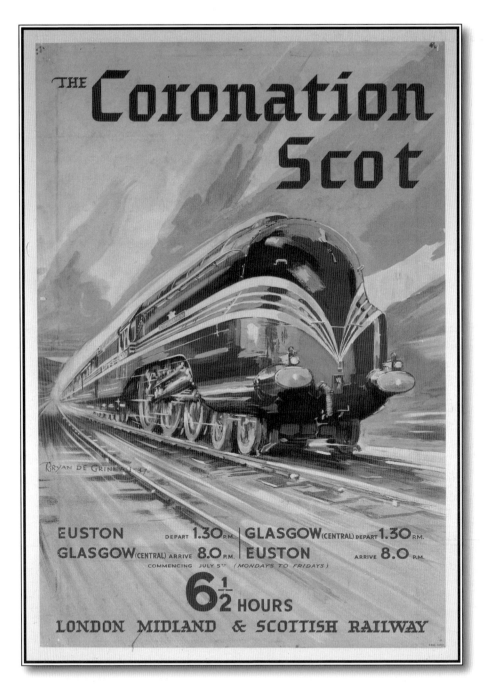

A late Thirties poster for the Coronation Scot, *the most glamorous train of the steam age to run through Cheshire.* (National Railway Museum)

Introduction

In terms of railway history, Cheshire differs from most other counties in one single respect. It is a county in which major lines were built to pass through, rather than to access particular local destinations. Yes, like all other counties it had and still has its own network of local cross-country routes and branch lines, but its biggest contribution to the national rail network lay in the development of major trunk routes linking London and the industrial West Midlands to Liverpool, Manchester and the North, and to Holyhead, the port for Dublin.

Cheshire took its role on the railway map to its heart, literally. For one of the great hubs of Britain's railway system was Crewe, not only a sizeable junction in its own right on what is now the West Coast Main Line, but the place where one of the world's greatest locomotive workshops flourished, and which proudly turned out some of the finest and fastest steam engines ever built.

All this, however, is a far cry from the days prior to the coming of the railways, when roads in the county were of very poor quality and major routes

Oil painting by Norman Wilkinson of Crewe Junction in the evening, in the 1920s. Wilkinson studied at Portsmouth and Southsea Schools of Art. As well as being a famous marine painter, he designed posters for several railway companies and organised the Royal Academy series of posters for the LMS in 1924. (National Railway Museum)

Before the coming of the railways, the Shropshire Union Canal, which somewhat mirrored the route of the later Grand Junction Railway, provided state-of-the-art rapid transport in Cheshire. At Barbridge Junction near Crewe, the Middlewich branch diverged from the 'main line'. (Author)

were few and far between. John Ogilby's map of 1675, part of his pioneering road atlas of England and Wales, shows a road to Chester via Whitchurch and another running through Nantwich and passing through Warrington and Preston on its way to Carlisle. Chester, the county town, was the focal point of Cheshire's road network and for centuries dwarfed Liverpool in importance: another route ran from the Roman city to Warrington, Manchester and York.

From the late 17th century onwards, a series of roads were built in the North-West, financed by travellers paying tolls to use them. They linked the region's rapidly-growing towns and cities which, by the late 18th century, were expanding because of the Industrial Revolution. Following the creation of the turnpike roads from Warrington to Preston and Liverpool to Prescot in 1726, until the mid-1880s, around 160 were built in Cheshire and neighbouring Lancashire.

Better transport, however, was needed to link the manufacturing towns to the great Merseyside port. In 1761, James Brindley's Bridgewater Canal, linking Runcorn to Manchester, was opened with such success, cutting the price of coal by half at a stroke, that it sparked off the great period of building artificial navigable inland waterways known as the Canal Mania. Later it was largely superseded by the Manchester Ship Canal.

The canal network played a major role in the Industrial Revolution, by facilitating the cheap and efficient shipment of raw materials to manufacturing bases and the finished products to new national markets. In turn, the great period of industrial and economic progress spawned the steam railway age, widely held to have begun in 1804, when Cornish mining engineer Richard Trevithick successfully demonstrated a working steam locomotive in public for the first time, on the Penydarren Tramroad near Merthyr Tydfil.

At this point I must thank those responsible for local government reorganisation in 1974 for making the narrative easier; for boundary changes saw Warrington moved from Lancashire into Cheshire, along with the parishes of Burtonwood and Culcheth and Glazebury. Both include sections of the world's first inter-city railway, the Liverpool & Manchester, which opened in 1829 and which set the pace for the way not only Cheshire's transport links but those of the entire world would soon be changed beyond recognition forever.

Because of these boundary changes, the Liverpool & Manchester Railway therefore comes within the scope of a book on Cheshire railways, and so we can begin at the beginning, as it were.

Robin Jones

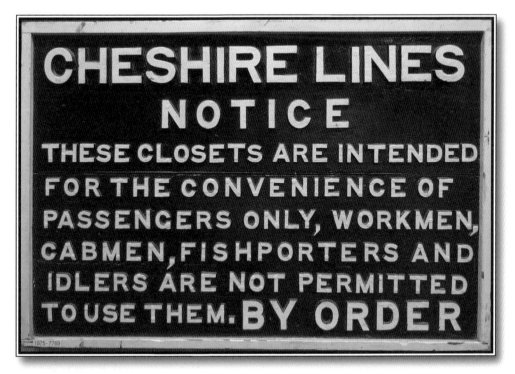

Idlers were not welcome in Cheshire Lines Committee toilets. (Author)

THE FIRST INTER-CITY RAILWAYS

The world's first public railway to use steam haulage was the Stockton & Darlington, which opened in 1825, after being engineered by George Stephenson. However, even then, the steam locomotive did not convince everyone that it was the future of transport: some still believed that the horse, the time-honoured method of traction, was more economical, reliable and safe, while others pointed to the use of cable haulage, great drums powered by stationary steam engines winding trains along.

Before it was given parliamentary permission in 1823 to build its line, the Liverpool & Manchester had played down the use of steam locomotives because of public fears that they would either explode, causing widespread carnage, or poison everyone with fumes.

That year, Stephenson and his son Robert visited William Locke and his son Joseph, then 17, at Barnsley. It was agreed that Joseph would go to work for the Stephensons at the locomotive works near Forth Street, Newcastle-upon-Tyne, which had been set up to build engines for the Stockton & Darlington. Locke quickly rose through the ranks to a position of authority despite his youth.

As Liverpool & Manchester directors continued to debate which form of traction should be used, in March 1829 Robert Stephenson and Joseph Locke produced a report arguing that locomotives were superior when it came to busy railways. As a result, the directors decided to hold an open competition to find the best locomotive. This contest took the form of the Rainhill Trials, held in October 1829. An early failure in the event was *Decapod*, a four-wheeled contraption powered by a horse running on a treadmill, while the winner was father-and-son team George and Robert Stephenson's locomotive *Rocket*, innovations in which established the blueprint for the future evolution of the steam locomotive.

The railway, which after a series of disputes ended up being engineered by George Stephenson with Locke as his assistant, included several groundbreaking engineering feats. There was the 2,250-yard Wapping Tunnel running from the south end of Liverpool Docks to Edge Hill, the world's first tunnel to be bored under a city; the 70-ft-deep Oliver Mount cutting through solid rock; and the world-famous, 4¾-mile-crossing of the great undrainable peat bog that was Chat Moss, floating the track on hurdles made from wood and heather. Even today, if you stand near the lineside, you can feel the ground move as a train passes, despite the fact that modern locomotives are 25 times the weight of the *Rocket*,

George Stephenson, builder of the Liverpool & Manchester Railway.

which hauled the first experimental train over Chat Moss in January 1830. While George Stephenson is credited with the Chat Moss crossing, many believe it was more the work of Locke.

Straddling the Sankey Brook which forms the modern-day boundary between Cheshire and Merseyside is the great nine-arch Sankey Viaduct in Burtonwood parish. Constructed from yellow and ginger sandstone and red brick, this Grade I listed structure was built by George Stephenson to cross the Sankey Canal with sufficient clearance for the sailing boats, known as the Mersey flats, which used it. Known locally as the Nine Arches, not only is it the earliest major railway viaduct in the world, but crossed the first canal built in the Industrial Revolution, and therefore is of paramount historical importance.

Due to the limitations of the track, set onto individual stone blocks without sleepers, the first Liverpool & Manchester Railway trains travelled at 17 mph, yet when the line opened on 15 September 1830, this was considered light-speed technology by local residents of the day. Drivers who travelled faster faced being reprimanded.

Another 'first' apportioned to the line was the world's first public railway

The National Railway Museum's modern-day working replica of Stephenson's Rocket *and open carriages in action.* (Author)

passenger fatality. On the opening day, at Parkside station, Liverpool MP William Huskisson, President of the Board of Trade and Treasurer of the Navy, fell beneath *Rocket* when trying to climb into the carriage of the special opening train carrying the Prime Minister, the Duke of Wellington, pulled by locomotive *Northumbrian*. He is said to have exclaimed, 'I have met my death – God forgive me!' *Northumbrian* was hastily detached from the special to take Huskisson to hospital – forming the world's first ambulance train – but he died in the vicarage at Eccles after making his will.

Despite this bad start, the railway was hugely successful. Within weeks it ran its first excursion trains, and carried the world's first mail by rail, as well as early road-rail containers for the removal company Pickfords. By the middle of 1831, tens of thousands of punters and sightseers were being carried by special trains to Newton Races.

The opening of the Liverpool & Manchester Railway, the world's first inter-city line.

In 1837 work began on upgrading the original track, the year after the 1,980-yard tunnel from Liverpool Lime Street to Edge Hill was completed. Worked in the early years without steam engines, carriages descended by gravity while controlled by brakemen and were hauled back up to Edge Hill by rope from a stationary engine. On 4 May 1844, the new Manchester Victoria station was opened, relegating the original Liverpool Road terminus to freight use.

It was the first major railway to use Stephenson's gauge of 4 ft 8½ in, which today is regarded as 'standard' gauge. His earlier Stockton & Darlington Railway, normally credited with that feat, used the slightly narrower 4 ft 8in gauge in its early years, chosen because it was commonly used in the Durham coal mines and so existing wagons could be run on it. For the Liverpool & Manchester, George and Robert added half an inch to reduce binding on curves.

The Liverpool & Manchester also developed the practice of red signals for stop, green for caution and white for clear. By the early 1840s it had spread to other railways in Britain and the United States, the colours later changing to the red, yellow and green of today.

A year before the Liverpool & Manchester Railway opened, work had begun on an even more grandiose scheme, the creation of an 82-mile trunk railway. The Grand Junction Railway ran from Dallam in Warrington, where it made an end-on junction with the Warrington & Newton Railway, a branch of the Liverpool & Manchester, via Warrington, Crewe, Stafford and Wolverhampton to Birmingham. Here it was to initially share Robert Stephenson's London & Birmingham Railway's Curzon Street terminus, thereby providing Cheshire's first rail link to the capital.

George Stephenson and Locke were the clear favourites to engineer what became the world's first long-distance railway. However, experiences with the building of the Liverpool & Manchester had highlighted the former's failings in

Birmingham's Curzon Street station, the 'halfway' point for Cheshire travellers to London, where the Grand Junction and London & Birmingham railways met. (Author)

organising major civil engineering projects, while Locke was renowned for his efficiency in this field. The Grand Junction directors hit on a compromise. They made Locke responsible for the northern half of the line and Stephenson for the southern half. However, it was no solution, for while Locke steamed ahead and had all his estimated costs completed quickly and contracts awarded, in the same period not one had been signed for Stephenson's section.

Again the directors tried to meet both halfway by making them joint engineers, but Stephenson's pride would not allow him to accept parity with his former assistant, and so he quit. By the autumn of 1835 Locke had become chief engineer for the whole Grand Junction Railway, to the great chagrin of Stephenson. Locke was now out on his own, but determined to show just what he could do in his own right. He decided to avoid major civil engineering works where possible, although they could not be done without altogether. The principal one was the stupendous 20-arch Dutton Viaduct, which crosses the River Weaver and the Weaver Navigation between the villages of Dutton and Acton Bridge in Cheshire, standing 60 ft high and 500 yards long.

The Grand Junction Railway opened on 4 July 1837, at first using a temporary station at Vauxhall in Birmingham before the 28-arch Birmingham Viaduct was built to link it to Curzon Street. The new railway quickly saw itself at the heart of a network. In 1840 it absorbed the Chester & Crewe Railway, just before that line opened. The Grand Junction had been designed as an 'A to B' railway, giving low priority to serving the

Joseph Locke, largely responsible for the Grand Junction Railway, who suggested moving its locomotive works from Edge Hill to Crewe.
(Author's Collection)

places en route – hence the fact that Wolverhampton was effectively bypassed. Had it been concerned with serving major centres in the Cheshire of the day, it might well have taken a route through Chester, but it was left to speculators to draw up plans for a branch line from Crewe, which until the coming of the railway was a mere hamlet. The Grand Junction also backed the development of the North Union Railway to effectively extend the line northwards to Preston, and invested in the Lancaster & Carlisle Railway and the Caledonian Railway.

The preceding years had seen the emergence of several railway schemes to carve up Cheshire with new inter-city lines. The Grand Junction looked at building a branch to serve the Potteries, while the Manchester & Cheshire Junction Railway planned a route from Manchester to Crewe, with several branches. George Stephenson produced a scheme for a Manchester South Union Railway from Manchester and Stockport to the Potteries. The net result was the Manchester & Birmingham Railway, which branched from the Grand Junction at Chebsey to run to a station at Manchester Store Street, with branches to Crewe and Macclesfield.

The first section, between Heaton Norris, and a temporary station at Travis Street in Manchester, was opened in 1840, prior to the completion of the great

The monumental 22-arch railway viaduct which dominates Stockport as portrayed in Victorian times. (National Railway Museum)

Stockport Viaduct today, carrying masts and overhead wires for modern electric trains. (GMAN)

22-arch viaduct which dominates the skyline of Stockport. Store Street, which was also used by Sheffield, Ashton-under-Lyne and Manchester Railway trains, opened in 1842 and later became known as London Road, changing to the more familiar Manchester Piccadilly in 1960.

Services were extended to Sandbach but there were protracted negotiations with the Grand Junction over access to Crewe. Agreement was reached whereby the Grand Junction would operate the trains south of Crewe, while the Manchester & Birmingham would run them into Manchester.

In 1841 the Grand Junction appointed Captain Mark Huish as Secretary. He had held a similar position with the Glasgow, Paisley & Greenock Railway. A ruthless and determined businessman, he played a major role in the company's fortunes, which soared to the point whereby in 1845 it absorbed its principal business partner, the Liverpool & Manchester Railway, and in conjunction with the Manchester & Leeds Railway bought the North Union Railway.

The Grade II listed Runcorn railway bridge, which spans the Mersey and the Manchester Ship Canal and links Runcorn to Widnes, was designed by William Baker for the Grand Junction Railway, but built for the LNWR and formally opened on 10 October 1868, the first passenger train running over it on 1 April the following year. Also known as Ethelfleda Bridge or Britannia Bridge, it comprises three 305-ft wrought iron spans and, replacing a centuries-old ferry, when built was the longest of its kind. (Peter I. Vardy)

The biggest step, however, came the following year, when the Grand Junction, London & Birmingham and Manchester & Birmingham all merged to form the London & North Western Railway, with Huish as secretary. From then on, it grew so big that by the late 19th century it was the largest joint stock company in the world. A plan to bypass the West Midland conurbation by building a line through the Trent Valley to Rugby had been placed on hold for financial reasons, but the merger produced sufficient capital for it to open in 1847, providing an even faster link from and through Cheshire to London. The historic amalgamation produced the West Coast Main Line, now one of the two busiest rail routes in Britain. Today we talk about building new high speed lines like the Channel Tunnel Rail Link 'in one go': in the early days of the rail network, such trunk routes came together in piecemeal fashion when adjoining railways decided to merge.

It is scarcely possible to overestimate the effect that the railways had on Cheshire which, despite its proximity to the great sea port of Liverpool and the manufacturing capitals of Manchester and the Potteries, was still very much a rural outback in the early 1800s. Before the coming of the railway, for instance, every town and village clock ran to its own time, which was almost certainly out of step with Greenwich Mean Time. The arrival of the railways allowed stationmasters to set their clocks by the watches of the train guards, and so standardise time with that of the capital.

The railways revolutionised lives in ways that few had dared imagine, and which we nowadays take for granted. Another major example is the postal service. A penny post delivering mail from Manchester to outlying towns such as Altrincham and Cheadle was running in the 1830s, but the cost of sending letters to London, and the time they took to be delivered by stagecoach, was much greater. While the turnpike roads had been a huge improvement on what had gone before, a stagecoach would take several days to travel from London to Cheshire and beyond. The railway reduced the travelling time to just a few hours and facilitated the introduction of the universal penny post in 1840. Later, Travelling Post Offices were introduced, with special apparatus for collecting mailbags suspended from lineside apparatus at speed and without having to stop.

Making mail delivery so cheap and efficient allowed letters to reach places well away from the old stagecoach routes. Towns like Chester, New Brighton, Runcorn, Macclesfield and Nantwich soon not only found they did not have to wait days to receive their post, but had the unheard-of service of deliveries twice a day and, in the case of Birkenhead, three times a day. By 1850, most villages had a small post office. The railways also made it possible for newspapers to arrive on the day of publication.

The availability of fast, cheap transport allowed inhabitants who had never travelled outside Cheshire in their lives to venture forth, looking for work or in later times, for excursions. The availability of rail transport and better pay and conditions drew many people from the countryside into the rapidly-expanding urban areas spawned by the Industrial Revolution.

Farm produce would never again have to rely on local markets, as cattle and cheese could be swiftly and comparatively cheaply transported over long distances, in special purpose-built wagons. While Cheshire was on the doorstep of Manchester and Liverpool, only now could those cities be supplied with milk from the county's farms in bulk for the first time. Rail freight also exported and imported cheap mass-produced household commodities and so on. More and

The interior of a LNWR Travelling Post Office, a type of carriage where letters were sorted in transit, used into the 21st century. Railways revolutionised postal deliveries in mid-Victorian times. (Author's Collection)

more coal began to be supplied for domestic use from railway stations rather than from canal wharves, cutting the price greatly. Such advantages came earlier to Cheshire than to many other parts of Britain because the railways had cut through the county, broadly following ancient routes from London to the North West and to Ireland.

The building of the railways not only provided much-needed work for local people, but brought in teams of labourers from beyond the county. These men, known as 'navvies' since the days of canal or navigation building, worked hard and played hard. They would shovel two tons of earth by hand a day, for which they might be paid two shillings – much of it being spent on drink in the evening. They lived in makeshift camps, and there was often verbal and physical conflict with the locals who found their presence overbearing.

Within two decades of the building of railways across the country, life in Cheshire had changed forever. The world had visibly shrunk. No longer was London at the far end of the country, at least a day's travel by stagecoach: the journey now could be made in just five hours.

2

THOMAS BRASSEY, CHESHIRE'S RAILWAY-BUILDING MAGNATE

Railway-builder extraordinaire, Thomas Brassey is to Cheshire what Isambard Kingdom Brunel is to the West Country.

A native of the small village of Buerton, south of Chester, at 16 he became an articled apprentice to land surveyor William Lawton and helped survey the new Shrewsbury to Holyhead road, now the A5. By the time Brassey reached 21, Lawton was so impressed that he decided to form a partnership with him, founding the firm of Lawton & Brassey in the Merseyside hamlet of Birkenhead, which then consisted of just four houses. The firm developed a brick works and lime kiln and ran several quarries on the Wirral. They supplied many bricks for the rapid expansion of Liverpool. When Lawton died, Brassey became sole manager of the firm.

Thomas Brassey, international railway builder extraordinaire.
(Author's Collection)

19

His first experience of civil engineering was the building of four miles of the New Chester Road at nearby Bromborough and the construction of a bridge over the River Birkett at Saughall Massie on the Wirral. He met George Stephenson, who needed stone to build the Sankey Viaduct, and together they visited Brassey's Stourton quarry in nearby Birkenhead. Stephenson suggested that Brassey become involved in building railways too. It was a fateful meeting – one that led to Brassey setting off on a path to becoming what many have described as the greatest railway builder in the history of the world.

After losing out on the contract for the Dutton Viaduct contract, Brassey was given the job of building the Grand Junction's Penkridge Viaduct between Stafford and Wolverhampton, along with ten miles of the track. He was so successful that doors began to fly open for the chance to build more trunk railways. When Joseph Locke designed a section of the London & Southampton Railway, he encouraged Brassey to tender for part of it, and again he won.

In 1838, Brassey won the contract to build the Chester & Crewe Railway with Robert Stephenson as engineer, along with the Glasgow, Paisley & Greenock Railway and the Sheffield and Manchester Railway, with Locke as engineer. He subsequently worked for Locke abroad on the Rouen & Le Havre Railway in 1844 and on several other lines, the longest of which was the 294-mile Orléans & Bordeaux Railway.

Back in Britain, in 1844, Brassey and Locke built the Lancaster & Carlisle Railway, providing a link from Cheshire to the Scottish border, including the

LNWR navvies at Stockport in 1890, having just widened Edgeley Viaduct.
(National Railway Museum)

Chester General station was a joint station between the Chester & Holyhead Railway, the Chester & Crewe Railway and the Birkenhead Railway. Dating from 1848, it was built by Thomas Brassey, with the Italianate frontage designed by Francis Thompson. It is one of only 22 Grade I and Grade II listed stations in England. The station has carved wooden owls in the roof beams to help deter pigeons. (Author)

legendary steep climb to the summit of the 916-ft Shap Fell with gradients as steep as 1-in-75; the above-mentioned Trent Valley line; and in 1845, the 85-mile Chester & Holyhead Railway. Cheshire's northern links were further expanded in 1845 when Brassey won the contract for the 125-mile Caledonian Railway, which connected Carlisle with Glasgow and Edinburgh. The following year he became involved with the building of the Lancashire & Yorkshire Railway between Liverpool and Hull, providing a trans-Pennine route with Cheshire connections. He also built 75 miles of the Great Northern Railway, now part of the East Coast Main Line.

In 1847, he started work on the North Staffordshire Railway, which entered Cheshire from the south. The Stoke-on-Trent-based company's main routes were built between 1846 and 1852, and ran from Macclesfield to Norton Bridge, north of Stafford, and from Crewe to Egginton Junction, to the west of Derby,

A LNWR long-boilered passenger locomotive sketched in 1852.
(Illustrated London News)

linking with the LNWR and other companies, and eventually extending to 221 route miles.

By the time that 'Railway Mania' ended in the economic downturn of the late 1840s, the one-time Wirral quarry owner had constructed a third of all the lines in Britain.

With contracts having dried up in Britain, Brassey was able to enjoy vast success in major railway building projects in Spain, Italy, Norway, France again, the Netherlands, the Crimea, and Canada, where the Grand Trunk Railway formed his biggest contract of all, with Robert Stephenson as consulting engineer. The line crossed the river at Montreal by Stephenson's 1¾-mile tubular Victoria Bridge, for which hundreds of thousands of components were made in Birkenhead or in other English factories to Brassey's specifications. When it opened in 1859, it was the longest bridge in the world.

Plaque fixed to the exterior of Chester station. (Author)

Brassey later built railways in South America, Australia, India, Nepal and Eastern Europe. Many of his British navvies followed him on his exploits round the world.

By the time he died in 1870, in St Leonards-on-Sea, Sussex, he had built five per cent of the world's total railway route mileage. Some said that his influence had exceeded that of Alexander the Great. He also built several docks including those at Birkenhead, and part of the London sewerage system for Joseph Bazalgette.

He is honoured by a bust in St Erasmus' Chapel in Chester Cathedral and another in the city's Grosvenor Museum, along with memorial plaques at the station. Chester's Brassey Street and Thomas Brassey Close are named after him, while in April 2007 a plaque was placed on Brassey's first bridge at Saughall Massie. In the village of Bulkeley, near Malpas, stands the 'Brassey Oak' on land once owned by the Brasseys, planted to celebrate his 40th birthday in 1845 and surrounded by four inscribed sandstone pillars.

3

THE WORLD'S GREATEST RAILWAY TOWN

Crewe has been described as the most famous railway town in the world. Yet it was created out of next to nothing by Joseph Locke and the Grand Junction Railway.

Back in the 1830s, a Nantwich solicitor bought 60 acres of land in extent, for £35 per acre, at Oak Farm, near the village of Coppenhall. It seemed a naïve purchase on his part. The nearest town was Nantwich, four miles away, and the local population was just 140, crammed into 27 houses. Nonetheless, the solicitor continued to buy more land until he owned about 200 acres. He made no attempt to develop the land, but wild rumours began to spread that it was to be sold on for railway use.

The rumours were right. The solicitor's land was bought firstly for the Grand Junction Railway from Birmingham to Liverpool, and then for the connecting lines to Chester and Manchester.

The basic, early station was built in 1837 next to a turnpike road in fields at Crewe Green, a separate settlement of just 70 residents, near to Crewe Hall, a Jacobean mansion built between 1615 and 1636 for Chief Justice Sir Randolph Crew. The name Crewe – which first appeared as Creu in the Domesday Book – was adopted out of courtesy to the current Earl of Crewe. Within three years, Crewe became a junction and the station was enlarged to cater for the additional traffic to Chester and Manchester.

The Grand Junction had looked at relocating its works to Winsford seven miles away, and Nantwich four miles to the west, but landowners rejected the proposals. Because of Crewe's unrivalled central position on its main line, at the point where the line to Chester diverged, the Grand Junction bought large parcels of land next to the station, from the solicitor, in 1840. It then moved its locomotive and carriage works from Edge Hill in Liverpool, to Crewe, building a new workshop in the 'V' space between the diverging lines.

The Grand Junction outshopped its first locomotive built there in October that year. A 2-2-2 tender engine outside-cylinder type with double frames and inclined cylinders which became known as the 'Crewe Type', it was named *Tamerlane* and numbered 32. Two months later, to mark the occasion, a sumptuous ball was held. A total of 422 'Crewe Types' were built between 1843 and 1858, in 2-2-2 form for passenger work and as a 2-4-0 configuration for freight, the latter becoming known as the 'Crewe Goods'.

A railway 'colony' mushroomed around the new works before Joseph Locke planned a 'new town' to house the workforce in 1843, again on land bought by this enterprising lawyer, by which time there were 200 houses, and about 800 men, women and children living in them. A total of 160 men were employed in the new works.

The Grand Junction built the civic Christ Church, which became the railwaymen's place of worship, and an associated school. Before it was built, a

Grand Junction Railway Locomotive Superintendent, William Barber Buddicom, established Crewe Works and then designed a new outside-cylinder 2-2-2 locomotive which was more reliable than the existing inside-cylinder engines. This is a scale model of the 2-4-0 version built at Crewe from 1846 onwards, and now in the National Railway Museum at York. (Author)

In 1845, 2-2-2 No 49 Columbine became one of the first locomotives to be built at the Crewe Works of the Grand Junction Railway. Columbine ran until 1902 and is now in the Science Museum. (Author)

clergyman held services in the works. Until 1897 the vicar, nonconformist ministers and schoolteachers received concessionary rail passes.

Its successor, the LNWR, went on to build thousands more houses, and also added churches and schools. It provided gas and drinking water supplies adapted from the works' own source, built a public baths, and staffed a doctor's surgery with a scheme of health insurance. The first police station in Crewe was built in 1854 by the railway, which also appointed its officers. That year, too, the railway opened a cheese market and a clothing factory for John Compton, who supplied the company uniforms.

The works expanded rapidly as it concentrated on locomotive building and repairs. In 1862, all locomotive work was transferred from Wolverton's railway works, which had been established in Buckinghamshire by the London & Birmingham Railway in 1838. In turn Wolverton became the LNWR's carriage works, while wagon building was moved north to Earlestown near Newton-le-Willows.

This move saw Crewe become the LNWR's sole locomotive works. The company's fleet grew from 949 locomotives to 3,100 in 1903. Crewe allowed the LNWR to become self sufficient in locomotive building, turning out every one of its engines until 1916, without the use of outside contractors.

In 1853, Crewe Works began making its own wrought iron. The first steel rails were rolled at Crewe in 1861, and the first locomotive boiler made of Bessemer steel was built there two years later. In 1864 a Bessemer converter for producing steel was installed at Crewe, which four years later became the first place to use open-hearth furnaces on an industrial scale, and was later equipped with a pair of electric arc furnaces. In a drive for self-sufficiency and economies of scale, it also had its own brickworks.

So from the outset, Crewe, which stands 158 miles north of London's Euston station, was the hub of the LNWR.

Traffic increased greatly with the arrival of the North Staffordshire Railway from Stoke in 1848 and the Great Western Railway lines from Market Drayton in 1863 and Wellington in 1867, adding a second route from the West Midlands. The GWR used running powers from Nantwich over the Shrewsbury-Crewe line built in 1858.

Crewe station can claim several world firsts. It was the first to have its own railway hotel, for instance: the Crewe Arms, built in 1838, is still very much in use. It was also the first to form a junction between more than two companies.

Passenger and freight traffic to and through Crewe soared relentlessly as the town spread across the surrounding fields. The original station was superseded in

In 1838, Crewe became the first railway station in the world to have its own hotel, the Crewe Arms, located directly opposite the entrance and still thriving today. (Author)

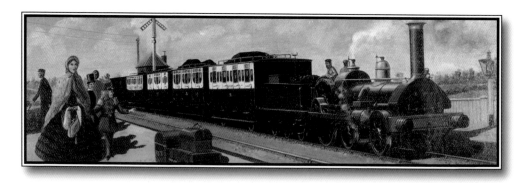

Travel in 1850 is an oil painting by Cuthbert Hamilton Ellis, produced in 1951 for a London Midlands Region carriage print, mounted above the seats in compartments to advertise other destinations. This one shows a LNWR first and second class train, hauled by the locomotive Courier, *passing Sandbach in 1850.*
(National Railway Museum)

1849 by a bigger version with ornate buildings and through lines in the middle. It was rebuilt again in 1861, the buildings facing each other on the present platforms 5 and 6 dating from this time. It was enlarged still further in 1867 with widened platforms and bays provided for local and stopping services.

In the 1870s, the LNWR purchased more land, to the south, for future expansion, which was required in the 1890s. By then, Crewe had become so busy as a junction that a survey showed 1,000 trains passing through within a 24-hour period, half of them freight trains that did not need to call at the station. Accordingly, the LNWR build a separate four-track 'bypass' railway to the west of the station, joining the existing lines beyond the north and south junctions, tunnelling beneath them and avoiding them completely.

This massive project also included a huge marshalling yard to the south of the station at Basford Hall with the capacity to handle 2,350 wagons, and a transhipment shed which facilitated the fast transfer of smaller loads from wagons to road vehicles under cover. There were 600 men employed to empty and load 1,100 wagons a day. The passenger station was also increased in size by 50% again with the building of a third island platform. In Edwardian times, an extra six platforms were opened. The North Staffordshire services from Derby and GWR trains from Wellington used south bay platforms, while the NSR ran summer excursion expresses from the Potteries to Llandudno through Crewe.

As locomotive power and speed increased, trains became longer and heavier. For much of the 20th century steam age, they continued to divide at Crewe with the front portion for Manchester and the rear for Liverpool. Express locomotives were often changed at Crewe, the 'midway' point between Euston and Glasgow.

A tank engine was delegated to act as station pilot, shunting extra vehicles on and off trains. There were always a pair of restaurant cars in a bay platform ready to attach to a morning service to London, and extra coaches to relieve pressure on overcrowded trains.

The massive station complex did not just deal with passengers, but a huge variety of freight, some of which had special needs. Live animals and birds, including pigeons for racing, were often despatched and received, and staff had to feed and water them as they travelled in luggage vans attached to passenger trains.

The first Locomotive Superintendent at Crewe was Francis Trevithick, the son of the man who had invented the steam railway engine. Born in 1812, he started studying civil engineering at the age of 20, and in 1840 was appointed resident engineer of the section of the line between Birmingham and Crewe. The following year, he was promoted to Locomotive Superintendent of the Grand Junction at Edge Hill works, and in 1843 was transferred in that capacity to Crewe. When the Grand Junction became part of the LNWR, Trevithick became Locomotive Superintendent of its Northern Division.

In the 1840s, as railways aimed to reduce travelling times by means of faster locomotives, the trend was for them to be built with a large central driving wheel, of around 8-ft diameter. Such large driving wheels would produce the high linear tyre speed needed for fast locomotives, while at the same time

The erecting shop in Crewe Works pictured in 1890. (Author's Collection)

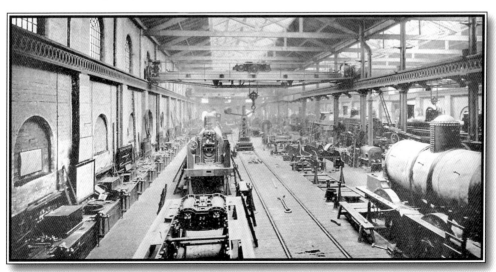

Francis Trevithick's pioneer Grand Junction Railway 2-2-2 Cornwall.
(Author's Collection)

keeping the axle bearing and piston speeds sufficiently low to remain within the technology limits of the day. Later on, increasing engine power would require better adhesion than could be achieved with single driving wheels, but that was not yet a problem at this time. However, the design needed a low centre of gravity, and early locomotives of this type accordingly were fitted with low-slung boilers. The problem here was that there was a conflict between the driving axle and boiler positions.

Engineer Thomas Russell Crampton overcame this by placing the single driving axle behind the firebox, so that the driving wheels could be huge. The net result was a long locomotive, often with a 6-2-0 wheel arrangement. One of the Cramptons supplied to the LNWR, Liverpool, could certainly work heavy trains at speed, but its long rigid frame resulted in track damage. Francis Trevithick solved the problem with the design of his 4-2-2 locomotive of 1847, No 173 *Cornwall*, named after his home county. He moved the driving axle ahead of the firebox, giving a shorter overall wheelbase and positioning the boiler beneath the driving axle. *Cornwall* was exhibited at the Great Exhibition of 1851.

In 1857, when the LNWR Northern and North Eastern divisions merged, Trevithick had to step down in favour of the latter's Locomotive Superintendent, John Ramsbottom, who took over at Crewe. Francis Trevithick's son Arthur Reginald Trevithick became assistant locomotive works manager at Crewe. After leaving the LNWR, Francis Trevithick returned to Cornwall and wrote a biography of his father which was published in 1872.

The son of a cotton mill owner who had worked for the Manchester firm of Sharp Roberts & Co, John Ramsbottom had been appointed Locomotive Superintendent of the London & Birmingham Railway in 1842. He invented the first reliable safety valve and the scoop used by express steam locomotives for picking up water from troughs between the tracks to avoid having to stop to refill the tanks. That in itself greatly speeded up journey times on trunk routes. In 1852 he invented the split piston ring, which provided a tight seal of the locomotive piston against the cylinder with low friction. He also improved tooling at Crewe and introduced standardisation of parts between classes. *Cornwall* was rebuilt to his 2-2-2 design in 1858, and in this form is now an exhibit in the Science Museum in London.

The same year, the first of Ramsbottom's DX class of 0-6-0 express goods locomotives appeared. By 1874, 943 of them had been built, a record for any single locomotive class in Britain. The figure included 86 for the Lancashire & Yorkshire Railway and two for the Portpatrick & Wigtownshire Railway.

The 2-2-2 Problem or Lady of the Lake class appeared in 1859, with

One of the most unusual steam engines to be seen around Crewe Works was this LNW 0-4-2 crane tank, No 3248. It had a working crane built into the back of the cab so it could lift items on to a truck behind. It is pictured at work on 27 August 1933. (Jarvis Collection/Midland Railway Trust)

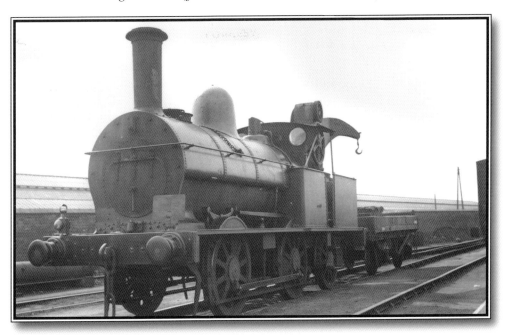

An aerial view of Crewe Works in 1928. (Author's Collection)

7ft 6in driving wheels. Like so many early locomotive types, they lacked both brakes and drivers' cabs: it is hard to imagine how the locomotive crews of the age struggled at speed in the worst of British weather, but succeed they did, and a total of 60 were built.

In 1863, Ramsbottom produced the 90-strong Samson class of 2-4-0 passenger singles. His Newton class of 96 2-4-0s which appeared in 1866 were a development of the DXs for passenger-working on the Lancaster & Carlisle line. No 1481 was named *Duke of Edinburgh* to mark the Duke's visit to Crewe.

During Ramsbottom's time in office, Crewe Works saw massive expansion and diversification and by 1870 was twice the size it had been a decade before. In 1868, the need for more space to expand Crewe Works necessitated the moving of the Chester line a short distance to the south. Ramsbottom was elected president of the Institution of Mechanical Engineers in 1870 and 1871, the year he retired from the LNWR.

By now, locomotive building by the LNWR had increased to the point where other manufacturers cried foul. In 1876, following the sale of ten 2-4-0 tender engines and 86 0-6-0s to the Lancashire & Yorkshire Railway, private locomotive manufacturers obtained an injunction to stop the LNWR producing anything but its own needs. This injunction remained in force until 1974, six years after steam haulage ended on British Railways!

THE 'KING OF CREWE' FRANCIS WEBB AND BEYOND

Between 1871, when the town's population had grown to 40,000, and 1902, Crewe Works was ruled by LNWR Locomotive Superintendent Francis Webb, later given the title of Chief Mechanical Engineer, whose influence extended far outside its gates. The choice of the world 'rule' is deliberate, as Webb, who produced 29 locomotive designs and a total of 2,366 locomotives, was referred to as the 'King of Crewe'.

By 1871, Crewe had become so big that it was incorporated as a town, with a mayor, aldermen, and town councillors. Webb, who had served as an apprentice under Francis Trevithick, was twice made mayor of Crewe, and also served as a Cheshire magistrate and alderman.

He introduced the design and building of compound locomotives to Crewe. A compound locomotive is powered by a

Francis Webb, the 'King of Crewe'.

type of steam engine where steam is expanded in two or more phases, the cylinders working in series as opposed to the arrangement of a simple expansion locomotive where they work in parallel. The advantages of compound locomotives include coal and water economy, greater efficiency through a higher power/weight ratio and better riding qualities with less wear on the track.

In 1873, he introduced the first of his Coal class 0-6-0s which, as the name suggests, were designed for hauling heavy coal trains. By 1900, 500 of them had been built. One of the Coal tanks survives, in the ownership of the National Trust, a body normally associated with historic houses and coastlines. Based on the Keighley & Worth Valley Railway, No 1054, which dates from 1888, is looked after by the Bahamas Locomotive Society.

The Cauliflower class of 0-6-0 freight locomotives appeared in 1880, with an 0-6-2T version coming out the following year. The Cauliflowers took their nickname from the LNWR's coat of arms, which was said to resemble the vegetable.

While he produced many splendid goods locomotives, it was Webb's passenger engines that earned him lasting fame. Best of all were the Jumbo or Precedent 2-4-0s that Crewe built between 1874 and 1882, when the first of his compound locomotives was constructed, the 2-2-2-0 Experiment class, followed by the Dreadnought class.

In 1889, Webb oversaw the construction of his most successful compound design, the Teutonics 2-2-2-0s. Three years later, he began the LNWR series of 0-8-0 compound freight locomotives, which in their day were the most successful goods engines in Britain, and were able to haul 940 tons south of Crewe. Webb and his successors modified the design on many occasions to produce several variations, and improvements to the type were still being made under British Railways half a century later.

In 1874 the LNWR began to manufacture its own signals at Crewe using a system devised by Webb, and this step led to yet another large influx of workers to the town. Eventually, the site boasted workshops for the manufacture of almost every article, big and small, that was required to run a railway.

In 1877, Crewe Alexandra FC was formed. The club is nicknamed the Railwaymen because of its close links with the town's main industry; many LNWR staff played for them in the early years before they turned professional. Also in 1877, the town marked the golden jubilee of both Queen Victoria's reign and the opening of the Grand Junction Railway, with the dedication of Queen's Park on land given to the town by the LNWR and laid out by Webb. That year, the works outshopped its 3,000th locomotive, No 600, a 2-2-2T compound.

Webb formed a Railway Engineer Volunteer Corps of LNWR workers and nearly 300 men served in the Boer War of 1899-1902. By that time, the company employed 10,000 people at Crewe, accounting for nearly a quarter of the population, and owned more than 1,000 cottages.

The centre of social life for the thousands of railway workers was the Mechanics Institute, which had been founded in the Grand Junction era. Classes were established for instruction in various branches of practical knowledge for apprentices and workmen.

By Edwardian times, the works extended for nearly two miles, the older section placed in the angle between the Liverpool and Chester lines, while the newer portions followed the Chester line nearly as far as Worleston, the next station.

The works had become so big that it needed an internal railway system of its own to facilitate production. It had been planned in 1857 by Ramsbottom and was a first in itself. Crewe's use of locomotive-propelled vehicles within a manufacturing plant impressed to the point it was quickly adopted elsewhere. Before the coming of the internal railway, built to the 18in gauge with special 'miniature' steam engines to haul wagons, most internal transport was carried out by hand cart and barrow.

There were four sections to the system built at different times, and much altered over the years before the narrow gauge tramway was finally abandoned. The first section began operating in 1862 within the original locomotive works. The second served the steel works section from 1864, again using locomotive haulage. A third section served the deviation works section and comprised an extensive but hand-worked tramway which lasted in service until as late as 1980.

The fourth section of the works tramway extended the system from the original works through to Crewe station. Built in 1878, it included the Spider Bridge, a typical railway footbridge providing pedestrian access from the works to the station and built on stilts and suspension cables for several hundred yards across the whole of Crewe North junction. The bridge carried the tramway down its centre to a footbridge which spanned the platform at the north end of the station. Goods for transfer between the works and the station were manhandled between the tramway and the station platforms via the footbridge steps.

Webb left a third of his large estate to found the Webb Orphanage at Crewe for the children of LNWR employees.

George Whale, who had entered the Crewe drawing office in 1865, took over responsibility for all LNWR engines in 1898, at the age of 55. He replaced Webb in 1903, and is best remembered for his Precursor class of 130 4-4-0s. The Precursors were a bigger version of Webb's LNWR Improved Precedents, but Whale used them to replace his predecessor's compounds which had proved

While Crewe Works built some of the world's most powerful steam locomotives, it also turned out some of the smallest, for its own use. Diminutive saddle tank Pet was built in 1865 for use on Crewe's internal 18-inch gauge system, and is now preserved in the National Railway Museum at York. (Author)

Billy was another of the tiny 0-4-0 steam engines built for use on the 18-inch gauge internal railway at Crewe Works. (Author's Collection)

Precursor No 5236 outside Crewe North shed in March 1933.
(Jarvis Collection/Midland Railway Trust)

unreliable. The Experiment class 4-6-0s were an extended form of the Precursor that appeared in 1905, with a tank engine version emerging from Crewe the following year. The last in service, No 25297 *Sirocco*, was taken out of traffic by British Railways in 1949.

Whale vacated his position of Locomotive Superintendent in 1908 and retired in June 1909 due to ill health. He died aged 67. He was succeeded as Chief Mechanical Engineer by Charles Bowen-Cooke. By this time there were numerous families in Crewe who had produced several generations of railwaymen.

Bowen-Cooke's main types included the 90 George the Fifth Class 4-4-0 steam locomotives, a development of Whale's Precursors, built between 1901-15, the last examples remaining in service until 1948, and the Claughton four-cylinder express passenger 4-6-0s. Introduced in 1913, the first of the 130-strong class No 2222 was named after LNWR chairman Sir Gilbert Claughton. The last was built in 1921 and the final one in service, No 6004 *Princess Louise*, was withdrawn by British Railways in 1949.

Bowen-Cooke was the first to add superheaters to LNWR locomotives. A superheater reheats the steam generated by the boiler, thereby increasing its thermal energy and boosting the efficiency of the steam engine. He fitted them to several of the Precursors as well as to his own designs.

LNWR Chief Mechanical Engineer Charles Bowen-Cooke.
(Author's Collection)

In those times, boys accepted into Crewe Works came in three categories: apprentices, premium apprentices, and 'pupils'. The first named were the sons of existing employees who kept up the great tradition of family involvement in the employment of the LNWR, taking that extra special pride in their work in building new locomotives. Premium apprentices were taken on payment of a specified premium and youngsters came from all over the country to join on this basis. They usually served until age 21, and were paid prescribed rates plus the normal piecework bonus for what was a hard slog.

Pupils, limited to six, were admitted from the ranks of the premium apprentices

Bowen-Cooke's Prince of Wales express passenger 4-6-0s were introduced in 1911, and out of 245 built for the LNWR, 135 were constructed at Crewe between 1911 and 1919. No 5625 is pictured at Crewe on 22 April 1933.
(Jarvis Collection/Midland Railway Trust)

No 5999 Vindictive, a reboilered example of Bowen-Cooke's Claughton four-cylinder express passenger 4-6-0s which were built at Crewe and introduced in 1913.
(Author's Collection)

Crewe Technical School where railwaymen were educated, pictured on a postcard in late Edwardian times. (Author's Collection)

and because of the small number allowed, there was usually a waiting list. A high annual fee was paid to the Chief Mechanical Engineer and the pupils received no pay until they arrived in the Drawing Office. Before then, they had to gain experience in as many workshops as possible. A pupilage normally lasted two years, after three or four years as a premium apprentice.

All would-be employees were taken through the works, usually with their parents, and saw for themselves what heavy railway engineering was all about. It is said that many never returned to the sweltering and fume-filled workshops, instead electing to study engineering at a university in far more palatable surroundings.

For the new boys, the working week was 54 hours, from 6 am to 5.30 pm, getting out of bed at 5.15 am, grabbing a quick breakfast and walking or cycling from lodgings to the works. They would return again at 8.15 am for a proper breakfast and again at dinnertime.

Some of the newcomers were allocated to the old nut and bolt shop, and in time-honoured works tradition, would play pranks galore, in the absence of the foreman. One favourite trick was to hide in a large bin and aim a nut at a youth on a bolt lathe. The missile was intended to hit the target on the elbow just as he was cutting the metal. However, such malpractices were more than compensated for by the kindliness and unlimited patience of the chargehands and the fitters, who would go to great lengths to teach the budding engineers all they themselves knew – a great part of the tradition of Crewe Works.

By contrast, many new hands quickly found that a great haze of secrecy enshrouded the question of metal mixtures. Specialist knowledge was closely guarded: in the foundry, the foreman kept his formulae in a little red book which he carried in his pocket, never even allowing anyone to overlook its pages. It was said that one day when he went away on holiday, he left it in the office drawer and one youngster found a key which would fit. Inside was the little red book and the finder copied out all the mixtures for the benefit of his workmates. The foreman discovered his loss when he reached Blackpool and made a special journey back for the book, but by then the contents were known to all and sundry, and the episode was a popular joke for years afterwards.

Bowen-Cooke died in 1920, and as CME was replaced that November by another former Webb apprentice at Crewe, Hewitt Pearson Montague Beames, who had represented Lancashire at rugby union and served in the cavalry during the Boer War before returning to Crewe. From 1909, he was Bowen-Cooke's personal assistant, and after a spell serving with the Royal Engineers' Railway Company with the British Expeditionary Force in the First World War, he became Chief Assistant and Works Manager, Crewe Works. He was appointed deputy CME in June 1919. During his short spell in charge, he produced just one new locomotive at Crewe, an 0-8-4T for use in the South Wales coalfields and also reboilered the Claughtons.

After the First World War, the government saw that the future of the nation's transport system lay in merging the smaller companies into four larger ones, with large-scale planning bringing vast economies of scale. Accordingly, the Railways Act 1921 enabled the 'Grouping' of most of Britain's railways into the 'Big Four': the London Midland & Scottish Railway, which included the LNWR and Midland Railway; the London & North Eastern Railway, which took control of the Great Central Railway; the Great Western Railway; and the Southern Railway. The Cheshire Lines Committee continued to be jointly owned, a third by the LMS and two thirds by the LNER. As far as the LMS was concerned, Crewe was given the job of building the bigger steam locomotives for the company.

At the start of the Grouping, the LNWR first merged with the Lancashire & Yorkshire. That company's CME, George Hughes, was placed in overall control.

LNWR 1P 2-4-2T No 6660 was built in June 1893 at Crewe, where it was pictured on 22 April 1933. It was also scrapped at Crewe in December 1947, missing out on British Railways ownership by a few days.
(Jarvis Collection/Midland Railway Trust)

When the LMS was formed in 1923 following other mergers, Beames was made Mechanical Engineer, Crewe, again overlooked for the top position of CME in favour of the older man. He was promoted to deputy CME in 1930, but retired four years later.

Hughes' main locomotive contribution to the LMS was the 'Crab' mixed traffic 2-6-0, with 175 out of 245 being built at Crewe from 1926 to 1932. Their nickname derived from their large highly-angled cylinders caused by a restricted loading gauge, leading to their unusual appearance. They appeared after Hughes had retired, to be replaced by Henry Fowler. Three survive in preservation.

Fowler, who had been CME of the Midland Railway, and who in 1919 had been made a Knight Commander of the Order of the British Empire for his war work, became deputy CME of the LMS in 1923. He was responsible for the LMS at first adopting the Midland Railway's controversial small engine policy, which saw Midland standard types often having to double head heavy freight trains because they were not powerful enough to pull them in their own right,

An early 20th-century official LNWR postcard of Crewe's signalbox, making much of the fact that it was electrically operated. (Author's Collection)

thereby wasting resources. Amongst his LMS designs were the 7F 0-8-0, an update of the LNWR G2 class 0-8-0, of which 175 were built at Crewe between 1929 and 1932.

Between 1930 and 1934, he also delegated Crewe to build several of the 52 express passenger Patriot or 'Baby Scot' 4-6-0s, a smaller version of the LMS Royal Scots which had emerged from Derby works in 1928, combined with the boiler from the Large Claughtons of 1912, and which were regular performers on the West Coast Main Line through Cheshire for decades.

Fowler was briefly replaced as CME in 1931 by Ernest Lemon who, within a year, was promoted to Vice-President of Railway Traffic, Operating and Commercial, leaving the door open for a man who would produce Cheshire steam's proudest hours.

5

CARVING UP THE CHEESE

With the huge expansion of Liverpool and Manchester in the 19th century, there were other railway companies who were determined not to let the LNWR have it all its own way. Cheshire, which stood in their way, and which was once served by only a few roads, would soon be bisected by three more major railway companies, the increased competition bringing more benefits to county residents and businesses alike.

FROM THE EAST

The Sheffield, Ashton-under-Lyne and Manchester Railway opened in stages between 1841 and 1845 between Sheffield and Manchester, via Ashton-under-Lyne. It superseded the canal route over the Pennines which took eight days to navigate.

Sheffield land surveyor Henry Sanderson came up with the idea of a rail link between the two towns in 1826, but failed to gather support until the building of the Liverpool & Manchester Railway made others sit up and think. Backed by Liverpool financiers, a prospectus for the Sheffield & Manchester railway was drawn up in 1830, with George Stephenson as engineer, but arguments over the route led to the scheme fizzling out. It was revived in 1835 when engineer Charles Vignoles, who had worked on the Liverpool & Manchester in its early stages, was commissioned to produce a new route, via Woodhead and Penistone. The resulting Sheffield, Ashton-under-Lyne & Manchester Railway received its Act of Parliament in 1837.

The line had been opposed by the Manchester & Birmingham Railway, but agreement was reached that the line from Ardwick would be shared northwards to a joint station in Manchester.

The scheme involved the building of the great Woodhead Tunnel beneath the

Pennines. After the first sod was cut near the western end of the tunnel on 1 October 1838, Thomas Brassey began work as contractor. The first stage of the line, between a temporary terminus at Travis Street in Manchester and Godley Toll Bar, opened on 11 November 1841. The following year, trains ran into Manchester Store Street (Piccadilly). Running through the north-western extremity of Cheshire, the line went through Ardwick, Gorton, Fairfield, Ashton, Dukinfield, Newton & Hyde, Broadbottom and Glossop, and reached Woodhead in 1844. Disaster struck on 19 April 1845 when labourers died when the viaduct being built in Ashton-under-Lyme collapsed.

The completed line to Sheffield was ceremonially opened on 22 December 1945, after the tunnel, then the longest in the country at two miles, was declared safe. Sheffield, Ashton-under-Lyne & Manchester Railway directors had originally hoped to connect to the Liverpool & Manchester Railway, but were turned down, and instead reached an agreement with the London & Birmingham Railway, which led to the formulation of plans for the Manchester, South Junction & Altrincham Railway.

In July 1846, plans to merge the Sheffield, Ashton-under-Lyne & Manchester Railway with the Sheffield and Lincolnshire Junction, the Great Grimsby & Sheffield Junction, the Grimsby Docks Company and the East Lincolnshire Railway, received the Royal Assent. The new company adopted the title of the Manchester, Sheffield & Lincolnshire Railway on 1 January 1847, and gave Cheshire key outlets to the east coast.

A Manchester, Sheffield & Lincolnshire Railway 'No Trespassing' sign.
(Author)

THE CHESTER & HOLYHEAD RAILWAY

The reason for the building of the Chester & Holyhead Railway dates back long before the invention of the steam locomotive, to the days of Elizabeth I. In 1572 she announced the launch of a weekly postal service to Ireland, using a road via Chester and Liverpool. Four years later, the route was amended in favour of Holyhead, which offers a shorter sea crossing. The service consisted of civil servants riding on horseback to convey messages between the British Parliament in London and their counterpart in Dublin. The service improved with the building of turnpike roads and by the 1880s a mail coach operated on a near-daily basis, taking 45 hours to reach Holyhead from London.

Thomas Telford's new road (now the A5) from Shrewsbury to Anglesey, including his Menai Suspension Bridge of 1826, led to travelling times being cut even further, to 30 hours. The Irish Sea crossing became quicker with the introduction of steam packet boats between Holyhead and Dublin in 1819, and shortly afterwards out of Liverpool too.

The building of the Liverpool & Manchester, Grand Junction and London & Birmingham railways combined with the steam packets from Liverpool saw the journey time from London to Dublin via Kingstown cut to 22½ hours. Accordingly, the coveted Irish Mail service was transferred to Liverpool. However, efforts were being frantically made to find an even shorter and quicker crossing, possibly via Porth Dinllaen on the Llyn peninsula, Newquay in Cardiganshire and Llandudno.

Holyhead understandably wanted its trade back, and plans for a Chester to Holyhead railway were first drawn up in 1838 and finally given Royal Assent on 4 July 1844. The double-track route included cutting through Chester's city walls, parts of which date back to Roman times, as well as walls at Conwy Castle, and building a sea wall at Abergele and a tunnel beneath the cliffs at Penmaenbach.

Nine of the company's 18 directors were nominated by the London & Birmingham Railway, three by the Chester & Birkenhead Railway and six by the Chester & Crewe Railway, which had become part of the Grand Junction. In 1844, the board dispensed with the services of George Stephenson and instead appointed his son Robert as engineer-in-chief. A Parliamentary Bill for the section of the route line Ogwen and Llanfair PG including a second bridge over Menai Strait was submitted. As we saw earlier, the contract for the line was won by Thomas Brassey in partnership with William McKenzie Ross and Robert Stephenson.

The first sod was cut at Conwy Tunnel on Saint David's Day, 1 March 1845.

The introduction of cheap transport by rail increased Chester's importance as a tourist destination, particularly with visitors from the USA arriving via the port of Liverpool, and many new hotels sprang up in the Roman city. The Queen Hotel opposite Chester General station was opened in 1860 and included Charles Dickens amongst its guests. Another important hostelry from this tourist boom was the Queen Commercial Hotel, now the Town Crier, which opened in 1867. (Author)

Stephenson's mind, however, was largely occupied with the building of the Britannia Bridge linking Anglesey to the mainland, in partnership with Scottish civil engineer, structural engineer and shipbuilder, William Fairbairn, its innovative design featuring wrought-iron box-section tubes to carry railway tracks inside them. The tubular design using wrought-iron to provide the ultimate in strength and flexibility had first been used on the line's Conwy railway bridge two years earlier.

When the Britannia Bridge opened in 1850, it was hailed across the world as an engineering marvel, having pushed forward the boundaries of railway engineering. However, one spectacular failure on the line was Stephenson's Dee Bridge near Chester, which had been completed in September 1846, and opened for local traffic after approval by the first Railway Inspector, General Charles Pasley.

Stephenson had designed it using cast-iron girders, each of which was made of three very large castings dovetailed together. Each girder was strengthened by wrought-iron bars. However, one of its three 98-ft cast iron spans collapsed on 24 May 1847 as a local train from Ruabon ran over it at about 30 mph and fell through, leaving three passengers, two mail coach drivers, the train guard and the fireman dead, and nine other people seriously injured. The *Illustrated London News* reported:

> The sudden shock and concussion rendered almost all the persons in the carriages totally insensible of their situation. One man, indeed, named Proud, recovered himself almost immediately; he found himself in a carriage turned upside down in the river, and, being fully sensible of the horrors of his situation, he exerted himself to the utmost, and succeeded in getting through the carriage window, whence he precipitated himself into the river, and swam ashore.

The aftermath of the Dee Bridge disaster. (Illustrated London News)

The train consisted of one first-class carriage, two second-class carriages, and a luggage-van; but it is stated that there were not more than two dozen passengers. The train was proceeding as usual along the line, had already crossed two of the arches, and was in the act of crossing the third, when, without one moment's warning, all the carriages were precipitated into the river, a depth of about 30 feet; the engine and tender, which had crossed the bridge, pursuing their course along the line.

The crash was heard at a great distance, and assistance was promptly on the spot, Mr. Jones, the house surgeon of the Infirmary, being very active in rendering every aid to the unfortunate sufferers. In a brief space of time four dead bodies were taken out of the river, and twelve or thirteen of the passengers, who were more or less wounded, were extricated from their perilous situation, and conveyed to the Infirmary.

It also reported that the guard, George Roberts, 'met an instantaneous death, having been precipitated from the top of the carriage on to the bank of the river, amid the falling ruins.'

The engine driver, a Mr Clayton, said that when passing over the third span from Chester, he felt the rails sinking beneath him. He instantly put on the steam, and then felt the carriages sever. The engine and tender cleared the bridge and reached the abutments on the Wrexham or south bank of the river in safety, but the jerk or wrench arising from this severance threw the tender off the rails, inclining it sideways towards the stone parapet. The tender was finally thrown somewhat on its side, and about three feet off the rails, on the east side; this shock severing it from the engine, the iron bar or hook connecting them being snapped in two. 'The stoker, whose name is Anderson, was by this shock thrown off the tender upon the rails, and the screw-jack from the tender falling on him, killed him on the spot,' said the report, which added that one of the deceased coachmen was found to have £150 – a fortune in those days – in his pocket.

At a local inquest into the tragedy, Stephenson was accused of negligence, because cast iron was known to be brittle in tension or bending.

The ensuing investigation was one of the first major inquiries conducted by the newly-formed Railway Inspectorate. A report compiled by lead investigator Captain John Lintorn Arabin Simmons, of the Royal Engineers, suggested that repeated flexing of the girder had weakened the bridge significantly. He discovered that the main girder had broken in two places, the first break occurring at the centre, while driving a locomotive across the remaining girders proved that they moved by several inches under the load.

Simmons claimed that Stephenson's design was basically flawed, and that the wrought iron trusses fixed to the girders did not do anything to reinforce them. The inquest jury agreed with him.

Stephenson argued that the locomotive derailed while crossing the bridge and the impact force against the girder caused it to break, but witnesses claimed the girder fractured first. An extra load of ballast that had just been laid over the track as a fire prevention measure may also have contributed to the fracture.

Following the inquest, a Royal Commission condemned the design and the use of trussed cast iron, which had been used to great effect in the Crystal Palace in London, in railway bridges. The Dee Bridge was later rebuilt using wrought iron.

Despite this setback, the Chester & Holyhead Railway began running passenger trains over the 60 miles from Chester to Bangor on 1 May 1848 and across the Britannia Bridge to Holyhead on 18 March 1850. The Chester & Holyhead Railway became part of the LNWR on 1 January 1859, and, now known as the North Wales Coast Line, still connects to the Dublin ferries.

THE GREAT WESTERN'S NORTHERN OUTPOST

When the name 'Great Western Railway' is mentioned, the destinations that immediately come to mind are Paddington, Swindon, Bristol Temple Meads, maybe the Dawlish sea wall, Penzance, and a host of other places in the West Country, followed by those on its routes in Wales. It is often overlooked that the GWR also pushed north, right through the heart of Cheshire, to Birkenhead, as a direct rival to the LNWR. Just as the GWR's Paddington-Penzance main line came about through takeovers of associated railway companies, much the same happened with the lines north of Wolverhampton.

On 1 July 1854, the GWR opened Wolverhampton Low Level station. It was the furthest limit of Isambard Kingdom Brunel's controversial 7 ft 0¼ inch broad gauge, which at the dawn of the UK railway network was a serious challenger to George Stephenson's 4 ft 8½ inch gauge. The GWR looked to push further north towards the Mersey, a prospect that alarmed its rival between London and Birmingham, the LNWR.

LNWR General Manager Capt Mark Huish effectively forced the GWR to lay a third rail over several broad gauge routes, so that the trains of other companies including his could run along them. He thought he had won the day, but the move had the effect of pushing companies like the Oxford, Worcester & Wolverhampton and the railways serving Shrewsbury firmly into the GWR camp. All of these lines were standard gauge, and it left the GWR with a large route mileage of mixed gauge, and therefore greater versatility than it had before.

The Shrewsbury & Birmingham Railway started out with support from the

London & Birmingham Railway, but lost it when the LNWR was formed. The section between Shrewsbury and Wellington was to be jointly built with the Shropshire Union Railways & Canal Company.

It opened throughout between Shrewsbury and Wolverhampton on 12 November 1849. Meanwhile, the Shrewsbury & Chester Railway came about through a merger in 1846 between the North Wales Mineral Railway, which had powers to run from Chester to Wrexham, and the Shrewsbury, Oswestry & Chester Junction Railway. The line from Ruabon to Saltney Junction, on the Chester & Holyhead Railway, opened on 4 November 1846, and from Ruabon to Shrewsbury on 14 October 1848.

In 1850, the Shrewsbury & Chester made an agreement with the Shrewsbury & Birmingham to handle through traffic between Birmingham and Cheshire, breaking the LNWR's monopoly. The ruthless Huish tried to threaten both companies, but when this failed he gained a majority on the management of Chester General station, and immediately barred the issuing of through tickets to Birmingham and Shrewsbury, even having the Shrewsbury & Chester booking clerk forcibly thrown out of the station along with his tickets.

Such action forced both Shrewsbury companies into an alliance with the GWR, which had its eye on the lucrative Birkenhead freight traffic. After Huish was finally defeated in 1854, both companies merged with the GWR on 1 September that year. The Birkenhead Railway was born as a result of the merger of the Chester & Birkenhead Railway, which opened on 23 September 1840, and the Birkenhead Lancashire & Cheshire Junction Railway, which had received powers in 1846. Its route from Chester to a point near Warrington opened on 18 December 1950.

The Birkenhead line was the scene of one of Cheshire's worst-ever train crashes. Nine people died and up to 40 were injured in an accident in Sutton Tunnel between Frodsham and Moore on 30 April 1851, the day of the Chester Cup at Chester Races. The opening of the new line had halved the travelling distance between Manchester and Chester by taking a route via Warrington instead of Crewe and so record numbers of racegoers turned out. It was advertised as the Direct Route to Chester Races and around 4,000 people gathered at Manchester Victoria on the morning of the races. The overcrowded trains struggled to reach Chester. It was said that passengers from one train comprising 50 carriages ended up having to walk part of the way, while others were hours late.

After the event, returning trains were also packed: one made up of 18 small carriages carried 900 passengers. Hauled by the engine *Druid*, it needed to be helped up the incline out of Chester by another, No 16. After the train gathered speed, No 16 returned to Chester to haul its own train, but rain had turned to sleet, and *Druid* was again in difficulties, the driver and the guard having to lay sand on the rails so that the wheels could get a grip. Facing a 1-in-264 gradient uphill in the tunnel beyond Sutton Weaver viaduct, the crew struggled to keep the train moving.

The train headed by No 16 had left Chester and with only 430 passengers on board had a much lighter load and soon caught up with the ailing *Druid's* train. When it was just 60 yards behind the first train, *Druid's* guard signalled to No 16 to pull up behind and give it a push. To little avail, as No 16's wheels also began to slip and in the middle of the 1¼-mile tunnel, the two trains slid to a standstill.

At this stage, a third train headed by engine *Albert* entered the tunnel, having left Frodsham station 14 minutes after No 16's train, with the crew totally unaware of the big problem that lay ahead in the darkness. *Albert's* driver suddenly noticed that the tunnel was full of steam and tried to brake, but it was too late. He collided with the rear of No 16's train. Five people were killed outright and four died later. The guard from No 16's train walked back with a red light and stopped the next train on the viaduct, as 1,600 people were marooned inside the tunnel in pitch blackness.

An inquest jury returned a verdict of accidental death, adding that the railway company should accept 'great blame'. A local legend relates that gold coins discovered in the tunnel years later were believed to have been the race winnings dropped by passengers on that day.

A report by Captain R.E. Laffan, who was appointed by the Commissioners of Railways, recommended that a station should be built at each end of the tunnel and that the stations should be connected by an electric telegraph. He also advised that all carriages passing through the tunnel should be provided with lights, and the interval of five minutes between trains should be increased.

The stations were built in line with his recommendations. At the Frodsham end the station was firstly named Runcorn, then Runcorn Road, and finally Halton. At the opposite end was Norton station, later replaced by Runcorn East station.

The GWR made a bid to take over the company in spring 1852, but after being rebranded as the Birkenhead Railway in 1859, it was transferred to GWR and LNWR Joint control on 1 January 1860.

Beyond Shrewsbury, GWR trains were therefore able to run on their own line to Saltney Junction near Chester, using running powers over the LNWR Chester & Holyhead line to reach the Birkenhead line, which ran to Birkenhead Woodside. From there, it was a short walk to Woodside Ferry, the landing point for ferries across the Mersey from Liverpool. The mergers had given the GWR access to the north-west's major port, right in the heart of its rival's territory. However, Chester nonetheless provided a stumbling block for the Swindon empire despite the running rights. The GWR expresses were faced with the choice of having to reverse at Chester, or use the avoiding line and bypass the city.

A 12-mile branch of the Birkenhead line from Hooton to Parkgate opened on 1 October 1866, and on 19 April 1886 it was extended to West Kirby where it met the Wirral Railway.

The 20th century would see many of the GWR's illustrious locomotive classes on the Birkenhead to Wolverhampton route. Its completion paved the way for many golden decades for lineside enthusiasts in Cheshire!

THE CHESHIRE LINES COMMITTEE

Another challenge to LNWR supremacy in Cheshire came from the Great Northern, Midland and Manchester, Sheffield & Lincolnshire railways. In a bid to gain inroads not only into the county but also Lancashire, they banded together to take control of four proposed lines in Cheshire. The net result was the Cheshire Lines Committee, which at 143 miles became the second largest joint railway in Britain, after the 183-mile Midland & Great Northern Joint Railway.

Cast-iron post marking the boundary between the Cheshire Lines Committee and the Manchester, Sheffield & Lincolnshire Railway. (Author)

Branded as the Cheshire Lines Railway, 55% of its network lay in Lancashire. The Cheshire Lines Committee came about because of an agreement signed between the GNR and MSLR on 11 June 1862. It was empowered by the Great Northern (Cheshire Lines) Act of 1863, with the Midland Railway joining the other two big companies under the provisions of the 1865 Cheshire Lines Transfer Act. The committee became an independent company in its own right under the 1867 Act, although its board was comprised of three directors of the three companies.

Much of the impetus came from railway magnate, Sir Edward Watkin, who by 1881 was a director of nine railways including the CLC. He is best known for turning the Manchester, Sheffield & Lincolnshire Railway into the Great Central Railway, with the building of the London Extension from Annesley to Marylebone, to the bigger continental loading gauge. As chairman of the MSLR, the Metropolitan Railway and the South Eastern Railway, he controlled railways from the south coast ports to the capital, the Midlands and the industrial north. He was also a director of French railway company Chemin de Fer du Nord on the opposite side of the English Channel, and one of his dreams was the building of a Channel Tunnel. If his plans had succeeded, it would have been possible in the early 20th century to have taken a train from Crewe, Chester or Northwich through to Calais or Paris. However, his scheme faltered after an initial pilot tunnel was begun, due to lack of finance and also political pressures.

For the past 2,000 years, Cheshire has been famous for its salt mines and the arrival of the railways helped to take production of this long-prized preservative to much wider markets. This is No 252 in British Salt's steam era wagon fleet, now preserved in the Scottish Railway Exhibition at Bo'ness. (Author)

The Cheshire Lines Committee's station at Greenbank in Northwich.
(Author's Collection)

The four railways which became the CLC were the Stockport & Woodley Junction Railway, the Cheshire Midland Railway, the West Cheshire Railway, and the Stockport, Timperley & Altrincham Junction Railway.

The Stockport & Woodley Junction Railway was authorised in May 1860 to build a 2-mile line between the two points to link with the MSLR's Woodley to Manchester line. It opened on 12 January 1863, operated by the GNR and MSLR.

The Cheshire Midland Railway was empowered in June 1860 to build a 12-mile line from Northwich to the Altricham terminus of the Manchester, South Junction & Altrincham Railway, which was jointly owned by the MSLR and LNWR. The Cheshire Midland opened throughout on 1 January 1863.

Authorised on 11 July 1861, the West Cheshire Railway ran from Northwich on the Cheshire Midland to Helsby, where it joined the Birkenhead Railway's Hooton branch. The GWR and LNWR were given running powers over it. The West Cheshire's main line opened on 1 September 1869, and short branches from Cuddington to Winsford and Hartford to Winnington began operating on 1 June 1870.

The Stockport, Timperley & Altrincham Junction Railway was incorporated by an Act of Parliament of 22 July 1861 to build a line from the Stockport & Woodley Junction Railway to the LNWR at Broadheath Junction and to the Manchester, South Junction & Altrincham Railway at Altrincham. This line was

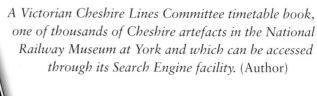

A Victorian Cheshire Lines Committee timetable book, one of thousands of Cheshire artefacts in the National Railway Museum at York and which can be accessed through its Search Engine facility. (Author)

opened during the winter of 1865/66 with another connection to the Manchester, South Junction & Altrincham Railway, at Timperley, opening on 1 December 1879.

The CLC received authority to construct a 34-mile line from a temporary station in Manchester to Liverpool, and it opened throughout in 1874. The company had its headquarters at Liverpool Central station.

The CLC had absorbed the Garston & Liverpool Railway in 1865 and used it as a section of the new main line. Manchester became the hub of the CLC network and as the MSLR and Midland Railway

Ex-War Department 2-8-0 No 90278, heads a freight train on the Cheshire Lines Committee route at Glazebrook, on the main line from Manchester/Stockport to Warrington and Liverpool on 21 June 1957. (Ben Brooksbank/Creative Commons)

was having to share London Road (Piccadilly) with the LNWR, it was decided to build a new terminus. Manchester Central was opened on 1 July 1880.

While the original Liverpool & Manchester Railway main line still operates as a secondary route between the two cities, the southern route, the CLC line via Warrington Central, is today the busier route. Starting with an hourly express service, its popularity mushroomed after it offered cheap fares between the two cities, increasing revenue by £10,000 within six weeks.

The Manchester, South Junction & Altrincham Railway

Running nearly 14 miles from Altrincham to Manchester's London Road (Piccadilly) station, the Manchester South Junction & Altrincham Railway was itself never more than a suburban line.

The line's enabling Act received Royal Assent on 21 July 1845. It opened between Manchester Oxford Road (the terminus for the first four decades) and

Heaton Mersey station, pictured in the 1920s, opened on 1 January 1880 as part of the Manchester South District Railway which linked Manchester Central to Stockport Tiviot Dale, and closed on 3 July 1961. From January 1889 until 4 May 1968, Heaton Mersey had a sizeable steam locomotive shed. (Midland Railway Trust)

Altrincham on 20 July 1849, while the South Junction sections from London Road to Oxford Road and from Castlefield Junction to Ordsall Lane were opened on 1 August 1849. The following month, the southern terminus was extended past Altrincham to Bowdon. On 3 April 1881 the original stations at Bowdon and Altrincham were superseded by a new midway station called Altrincham and Bowdon. When the line was built, it ran through rural areas largely concerned with market gardening, with Altrincham then just a small market town.

One big drawback of this line was that the joint owners often disagreed to the point where independent arbitration had to be sought. While the railway had its own coaches, locomotives were supplied by both the LNWR and MSLR. The railway kept three classes of passenger travel long after most other companies had eliminated second class.

The steam age ended early on this line. In order to fight back against increased competition from electric street tramways, the successors to the LNWR and the Great Central, the London, Midland & Scottish Railway and the London & North Eastern Railway, formed a Manchester, South Junction & Altrincham Railway Committee to look at electrification. In the late 1920s, 22 three-car LMS-design electric multiple units were built by Metropolitan-Cammell, and a depot for them was created on the site of the old Bowdon station. The first electric trains ran on 11 May 1831, and proved so popular that passenger numbers soared by 89% in the first five years. Publicity material labelled the 'new' 1500V railway as 'Many Short Journeys and Absolute Reliability'.

THE MACCLESFIELD, BOLLINGTON & MARPLE RAILWAY

Two railways arrived in Macclesfield on 19 June 1849: the LNWR line from Manchester, and the North Staffordshire Railway route from Norton Bridge via Stoke-on-Trent and Congleton. A new joint station, managed by a committee of both companies, was opened in Macclesfield at Hibel Road a month later, replacing the temporary LNWR station at Beech Bridge.

However, relations between the two companies would not always be that amicable. In 1869, the Manchester, Sheffield & Lincolnshire Railway and the NSR jointly opened the ten-mile Macclesfield, Bollington and Marple Railway. It was intended as an alternative route between Manchester and places south of Macclesfield.

Back in the 1840s, the NSR had started seeking a new route between the two towns that was independent of the LNWR. Because that company insisted on

Today's Macclesfield station was originally built by the Macclesfield, Bollington & Marple Railway and known as Macclesfield Central. (Author)

NSR traffic going via Crewe, the journey was longer and higher mileages were charged. The solution came in 1863 when Macclesfield entrepreneur Thomas Oliver aimed to revive Bollington's cotton industry by building a line from Macclesfield through the village to Marple, where it would connect with the MSLR. The MSLR was delighted, and had visions of the line extending south from Cheshire, maybe even as far as London.

Powers to build the line were obtained in 1864, and after building started, the LNWR reached agreement with the NSR over its Manchester-bound traffic. The NSR then lost interest in an independent route to Manchester. The line was built to single track and opened on 2 August 1869 for passengers and on 1 March the following year to goods. It was doubled in 1871.

6

RAILWAYS ON THE WIRRAL PENINSULA

Almost a county within a county, the Wirral peninsula that lies between the rivers Dee and Mersey was carved up by the Birkenhead, Mersey and Wirral railways, mainly providing services to overspill towns and extra port and manufacturing facilities for the Liverpool conurbation, not to mention a holiday resort or two. These made the growth of suburbia west of the Mersey possible.

The first steam ferry service across the Mersey started in 1817, paving the way for steamships to open up the west bank of the Mersey to industrialisation. John Laird opened his famous shipyard in Birkenhead in the 1820s and it was subsequently expanded by his son, William. The Lairds commissioned the architect James Gillespie Graham to design Birkenhead as a new town. The improved communications with Liverpool allowed city merchants to buy up large tracts of land for development in the Wirral. They included James Atherton and William Rowson, who developed the resort of New Brighton. Birkenhead's first docks and its municipal park, the first in Britain and the inspiration for New York's Central Park, opened in 1847.

The first railway serving the Wirral arrived in 1840 in the form of George Stephenson's 15-mile Chester & Birkenhead Railway, using a route chosen in preference to one of 18 miles passing through Willaston and Ledsham, and with fewer and lower gradients. The Chester & Birkenhead Railway Company was incorporated in 1837, but its first attempt for an enabling Act of Parliament was thrown out after eleven days of hearings that spring. A second Bill placed before Parliament also encountered difficulties but was passed later the same year. Opposition arose as different railway companies vied for access to the Merseyside ports.

Building began in May 1838. Trouble quickly flared amongst railway navvies at Sutton near Ellesmere Port when a wages clerk vanished along with their wages. A mass brawl between English and Irish navvies ensued, and 200 soldiers were needed to restore order.

The single-track line was officially opened in September 1840. The aptly-named locomotive *The Wirral* departed Grange Lane (later Road) station in Birkenhead and took 50 minutes to reach Chester's Brook Street, where cottages were doubling up as a temporary station until Chester General opened in 1848. In the first month, 10,000 passengers rode on the line. In 1840, in what may well have been the last gasp of horse-drawn road services, a race was held between a stagecoach and a train from Tranmere to Chester. The stagecoach was given an hour's start but still lost. By 1847 most of the line had been doubled, and in 1902, doubled again to provide four tracks.

From 1857, express passenger services ran from Birkenhead to Birmingham, and to Paddington from October 1861. The Irish Mail also used the route before the Chester-Holyhead route opened. By the mid-1880s, there were 22 passenger trains each day. However, freight gained ascendancy as the main source of revenue, and there were twice as many goods trains as passenger ones.

The line came under the joint control of the LNWR and GWR on 20 November 1860. Coal traffic from South Wales via the GWR was a prime commodity, with nearly 30 trains a day running over the line until coastal shipping took away much of this trade in the 1890s. Other imports to Birkenhead were building materials and manufactured goods, with grain, flour, fertiliser and even iron ore from Canada going south.

The Birkenhead Railway opened a branch line from Hooton to Parkgate in 1866, completing an extension to West Kirby in 1886. Its stations included Kirby Park, built of timber as a design experiment and mainly used as a halt for the nearby Calday Grange Grammar School. While this branch was an early closure casualty, with most of the stations being axed on 5 July 1954, Kirby Park remained in use by the school for another two years. The line was kept open for goods traffic and driver training until 7 May 1962 and is now the Wirral Way footpath and part of Wirral Country Park.

The Wirral Railway received Parliamentary powers in 1863 as the Hoylake Railway. It was authorised to construct lines from Birkenhead to New Brighton on the east side of the Wirral and Parkgate on the west, but only the former was built. Renamed the Wirral Railway in 1882, its lines ran from Birkenhead Park to the pocket seaside resort of West Kirby, with branches to New

Birkenhead Park station was opened on 2 January 1888 as a joint station between the Wirral Railway and the Mersey Railway and served as an interchange for the latter's new line to central Liverpool. This, the first station seen in Edwardian times, was destroyed by a bomb during the Second World War. The name is taken from the nearby park, which was the model for New York's Central Park.

Brighton and Seacombe, totalling 13½ miles in all. They mainly carried passengers, commuters to work and day trippers to the seaside. The stations were spaced very close together to serve the maximum number of people at a time when the urban sprawl of Liverpool was spreading across to the Wirral.

Great Central Railway trains on the route from Wrexham to Bidston ran over the Wirral Railway route to Seacombe, thereby giving a direct connection by ferryboat to Liverpool. A freight train served the coal depots at Moreton, Hoylake and West Kirby, a gas works at Hoylake and the Cadbury chocolate factory at Moreton.

The only fatal passenger accident on the Wirral Railway occurred at Birkenhead Park station on 6 December 1922, when a late train departing for West Kirby collided with an incoming service. Twelve people were also injured.

'Travel in 1895' is an oil painting by Cuthbert Hamilton Ellis produced in 1951 for a London Midland Region carriage print. It depicts a Wirral Railway train on the way to Birkenhead in 1895. (National Railway Museum)

Birkenhead North station was built by the Wirral Railway, replacing its earlier terminus at nearby Wallasey Bridge Road which had opened in 1866. It was originally known as Birkenhead Docks and opened on 1 April 1878. The LMS renamed the station Birkenhead North in 1926, and electrified the line through Birkenhead North in 1938, allowing through services to Liverpool via the Mersey Tunnel. (British Railways)

The Wirral Railway became part of the LMS at the Grouping of 1923. The LMS introduced a once-daily through train from New Brighton to Euston via Bidston and West Kirby, leaving after breakfast and returning in the evening. It was withdrawn in 1939 with the outbreak of the Second World War and never reinstated.

In 1886, the Mersey Railway opened to huge success. It linked Birkenhead and Liverpool, leading to further rapid expansion of both, and included the first tunnel built under the River Mersey. Entering Liverpool from the opposite direction to the Liverpool & Manchester Railway, it formed the second oldest urban underground railway network in the world after the London system.

The railway was built by contractor John Waddell, while the tunnel was designed by Sir Charles Fox, who had been a driver on the Liverpool & Manchester: indeed, as an apprentice he drove *Novelty* when it entered the Rainhill Trials of 1829. It was built by his son Douglas Fox, joint engineer to the Mersey Tunnel Company (set up in 1866) with James Brunlees. Douglas Fox was later involved with the construction of the Snowdon Mountain Railway, Britain's only Swiss-style steam-operated, rack-and-pinion line; the

The carving up of the Wirral by railways helped the growth of its seaside resort of New Brighton, a popular destination for Liverpool daytrippers via the Mersey Tunnel. (Liverpool Museum)

THE PIER, NEW BRIGHTON.

extension of the Great Central Railway from Rugby to London including Marylebone station; several of London's early underground lines; and the Liverpool Overhead Railway, the first electric elevated city railway in the world. For his work on the Mersey Tunnel, he was knighted by the future King Edward VII.

The first section of the Mersey Railway opened between Green Lane station in Birkenhead and James Street station in Liverpool. There were intermediate Birkenhead stations at Birkenhead Central and Hamilton Square, which were built so deep down that lifts were needed to access them. A branch to Birkenhead Park station opened in 1888, with a cross-platform connection with the Wirral Railway. In 1891, the Mersey Railway was extended from Green Lane to Rock Ferry, linking to the Birkenhead Railway. The tunnel was extended from James Street to a new Low Level station at Liverpool Central in 1892, giving a total length of just over 3 miles. Needless to say, it was a huge success, and by 1890, ten million passengers a year travelled through it.

Steam engines and long tunnels do not make good bedfellows. Where tunnels burrow beneath land, ventilation shafts carry smoke away, but underwater it is a different matter. The Manchester firm of Beyer Peacock supplied eight special 0-6-4T tank engines to haul the initial services on the Mersey Railway. They were fitted with pipes running down either side of the boiler, called condensers, to contain the steam exhaust as they passed through the tunnel. One of them, No 5 *Cecil Raikes*, named after Henry Cecil Raikes, MP for Preston in 1882, is preserved as part of the Liverpool Museum's collection. Beyer Peacock supplied another 0-6-4T, followed in 1887-8 by six 2-6-2Ts.

The Mersey Railway facilitated the speedy expansion of suburbs along its lines in the Wirral, such as Wallasey, Hoylake, West Kirby, Bebington and Heswall. Wallasey's population expanded to more than 53,000 by 1901, and its size caused by the availability of rapid transit links saw it obtain borough status.

The Mersey Railway began the demise of steam in Cheshire six decades before the rest of the county followed. In 1903, it became the world's first underground to switch totally from steam to electric power, following in the wake of the Liverpool Overhead Railway, which had run electric trains since it opened a decade before.

The Mersey Railway electric trains ran from Liverpool Central to Birkenhead Park and to Rock Ferry, where passengers changed on to time-honoured steam services for journeys beyond. Electrification of the Wirral Railway had been considered as early as 1900, and a contract for conversion was signed with Westinghouse in 1903, only to be cancelled through lack of finance. However, in 1938 the LMS electrified the lines from Birkenhead Park to New Brighton and

CHESHIRE RAILWAYS

Cecil Raikes was one of the Mersey Railway steam locomotives built in 1885 and fitted with condensing apparatus to pass through the Mersey Tunnel. It is now part of the Liverpool Museums collection. (Liverpool Museums)

to West Kirby with government assistance, and provided trains which gave a direct service to Liverpool. The railway and tunnel today form part of the Wirral Line of the Merseyrail commuter rail network.

Painted signage on the brickwork of Birkenhead Central station, which housed the headquarters of the Mersey Railway.

THE RACES TO THE NORTH

Running a major trunk railway through Cheshire was one thing. Turning it into a racetrack was another. By late Victorian times, train travel had become an accepted part of everyday life, and it was no longer a novelty to complete a journey that had once taken several days by road in just a few hours. Emphasis shifted to how quickly that journey could be undertaken. The Race to the North is the name historians have given to the competition between rival railway companies trying to outdo each other in terms of getting from London to Scotland in the quickest time, over the country's two principal trunk routes, the East and West Coast main lines.

The first Race to the North took place in the summer of 1888, between daytime trains from London to Edinburgh. The second was in summer 1895, and involved night expresses running between London and Aberdeen, with the finishing post being Kinnaber Junction, 38 miles south of Aberdeen, where the Caledonian Railway and the North British Railway routes joined. The two routes ran either side of Montrose Basin on the approach to the junction, and journalists covering the races could enjoy the spectacle of one train racing against the other.

On 20 August, the Great Northern Railway's Stirling Single 4-2-2 No 668 took the East Coast express 105.5 miles from King's Cross to Grantham in 1 hour 41 minutes with an average speed of 62.7 mph. An engine change saw No 775 take over, and complete the 82 miles to York in 1 hour 16 minutes, an average speed of 64.7 mph. The overall 393-mile trip was covered in 6 hours 19 minutes, at a speed of 63.5 mph, while the extended run to Aberdeen, making a total of 523 miles, took 8 hours 40 minutes, with an average speed 60.4 mph.

The LNWR responded two days later, and a storming run by Improved Precedent or 'Jumbo' express passenger 2-4-0 No 790 *Hardwicke* took 2 hours

LNWR Improved Precedent express passenger 2-4-0 No 790 Hardwicke *and its driver pictured in 1895, when it set a new speed record in the Races to the North.* (Author's Collection)

and 6 minutes to cover the 141 miles from Crewe to Carlisle with an average speed of 67.1 mph, setting a new speed record in the Races to the North.

The Improved Precedents were designed by Francis Webb and built at Crewe Works; 166 in batches between 1887 and 1897, and two more in 1898 and 1901. Officially, they were rebuilds of earlier types, the 96 Newtons and the 80 Precedents, but in effect this was done merely as a paper exercise for the accountants, and they were new-builds in all but name. However, they kept the names and numbers of the locomotives they replaced.

One such race in 1895 saw both trains reach Kinnaber Junction at the same time. The Caledonian signalman sportingly decided to let the rival North British train through, and it reached Aberdeen in 8 hours 40 minutes from King's Cross, compared to the standard 12 hours 20 minutes before the races began. The following night, the West Coast Main Line companies responded by making an 'exhibition run' from Euston via Crewe to Aberdeen in 8 hours 32 minutes. Again, the world was getting smaller, and events in far-off Scotland were reaping big benefits for transport links in Cheshire.

A reality check occurred on 13 July 1896 with a serious derailment on a tight curve at Preston, when a Euston to Glasgow train passed through the station at around 45 mph, ignoring the 10 mph speed limit, and leaving one person dead. The incident led to public demands for an end to staged train racing and more emphasis placed on safety. Also, passengers found that they were arriving at Aberdeen much earlier than the scheduled breakfast time of 7 am and had to wait on the empty station before connecting trains could arrive. So the rivals reached an agreement on speed limits.

SCOTCH EXPRESS APPROACHING CREWE.

An official 1904 LNWR postcard of a train labelled the 'Scotch Express' approaching Crewe. (Author's Collection)

Such was the public fear of trains running at too high a speed that when the Great Western Railway's No 3440 *City of Truro* allegedly became the first in the world to break the 100mph barrier, touching 102.3 mph with the 'Ocean Mails' on Welling Bank in Somerset in May 1904, the company kept quiet about it for many years.

The old rivalries were therefore suppressed, but never went away. While adhering to the agreement, the GNR's successor, the LNER, launched the famous non-stop *Flying Scotsman* express from London to Edinburgh in 1927, using special tenders with corridors which allowed engine crew changes at speed. However, the LNWR's successor, the LMS, stole a march on the LNER by running its own non-stop trains over the 401 miles from London via Crewe to Glasgow using one of the new Royal Scot 4-6-0s, and the 399-mile London to Edinburgh behind a standard Compound 4-4-0, both with volunteer crews. The old agreement on speeds was finally torn up in 1932, the year when a new CME was appointed at the LMS in the form of a man who would take the company, Crewe, and Cheshire steam to new dizzy heights.

Sir William Arthur Stanier (27 May 1876 – 27 September 1965) was born in Swindon, where his father was chief clerk to GWR Chief Locomotive Engineer,

The new erecting shop at Crewe Works in 1928. (Author's Collection)

William Dean. He followed in his father's footsteps, joining the GWR as an office boy in 1891 and then becoming an apprentice. By 1902, he had been promoted to Swindon Works Manager.

The LMS had become dissatisfied with Fowler's small engine policy and wanted new, modern and far more powerful locomotive designs. LMS chairman Sir Josiah Stamp approached Stanier because of his expertise with the GWR classic locomotives of the day, including the King and Castle 4-6-0s. Stanier was duly appointed as Chief Mechanical Engineer of the LMS from 1 January 1932.

One of his most successful designs of all was the 'Black Five' mixed traffic 4-6-0, which many locomen have described as the best all-purpose steam engine ever to run on Britain's railways. Here, Stanier drew much from the design of the GWR Halls, which could be seen regularly running to Birkenhead. Out of a total of 842 built between 1932 and 1951, 241 were constructed at Crewe. The class was so successful that several were still running up to the end of British Railways steam haulage in August 1968, and 18 have been preserved.

Between 1934 and 1936, alongside the 'Black Five' production line, Crewe built many of Stanier's 191 Jubilee main line passenger 4-6-0s, sharing the workload with Derby and the North British Locomotive Company. The last five of Fowler's Patriots had Stanier's taper boiler added and became Jubilees. The

This 'Black Five' 4-6-0 heading a passenger express out of a tunnel below Chester for North Wales was built at Crewe Works in 1948 and was one of 20 fitted with Caprotti valve gear, giving it a markedly different appearance to Stanier's originals which had Walschaerts valve gear.
(Eric Treacy/National Railway Museum)

class took its name from No 5642 *Silver Jubilee*, named to commemorate the Silver Jubilee of King George V in 1935. Four survived into the heritage era.

Stanier's 8F 2-8-0s, a goods version of the 'Black Five', of which 852 were built at many works, including 137 at Crewe, became a byword for freight haulage. With numerous examples exported overseas by the War Department, they became known as the locomotive that helped win the Second World War, during which the other three 'Big Four' companies also produced them. Ten Stanier 8Fs survive in preservation, with others known to exist in Turkey and Iraq, and at least two on the ocean bed off Egypt after the ship carrying them was sunk during the war.

In 1933, the launch of the 'Flying Hamburger' high-speed diesel railcar set in Germany grabbed headlines and led to British companies wondering how to emulate its success. The LNER decided that diesel power was not yet the way ahead, and in the right circumstances, steam could do the high-speed job just as well. Accordingly, a test run on 30 November 1934 saw modified A1 (later A3) Pacific No 4472 *Flying Scotsman* officially hit 100 mph, the first steam locomotive in the world to do so, on a run between London and Leeds. Far from playing down the feat, the LNER publicity machine rolled into action. The run was followed by A3 Pacific No 2750 *Papyrus* setting a new world record with 108 mph between London and Newcastle.

The streamlined A4 Pacifics designed by LNER Chief Mechanical Engineer Sir Nigel Gresley – who in 1893 had been apprenticed as a premium pupil of Francis Webb at Crewe – were built specifically to haul the new fast King's Cross to Newcastle and 'Silver Jubilee' services, with 112 mph reached by No 2509 *Silver Link* on the inaugural run on 29 September 1935. This new record began a fast and furious competition between the LMS and Crewe Works and the LNER to design and build even faster locomotives. The Race to the North was back on.

For many people in Cheshire, and indeed everywhere else, this was steam's finest hour. They had a grandstand view of the proceedings, but they also made it happen, by building magnificent new express passenger engines at Crewe Works and further underlining its capacity for world-beating technology.

DRIVER TOM CLARK: THE BOYS OWN LEGEND

Long ago, decades before the advent of TV and the internet, there was a celebrity culture in Britain. Back in the 1930s, for many the zenith of the steam era, short-trousered schoolboys did not idolise pop stars, film stars or multi-millionaire footballers, but engine drivers. In an age short of social media like Facebook and Twitter, they were the popular heroes who fired not only express passenger locomotives but every boy's imagination. They all wanted to grow up and become engine drivers – never mind the at-best average pay, long hours and dirty conditions.

Back in 1936, top of the steam celebrity charts was driver Tom Clark, a Crewe man whose exploits caused the whole nation to marvel. Clark joined the LNWR in December 1888 and worked through the links from cleaner to driver at 5A Crewe North shed, giving a lifetime of sterling service. However, his fame came in the twilight years of his career.

By 1936, when the LMS renewed their ancient rivalry with the East Coast Main Line operator, Stanier had already built a class of 13 new express passenger Pacific locomotives at Crewe Works. They were known as the Princess Royal class because each of them was named after a princess: built to haul the 'Royal Scot' train from Euston to Glasgow Central, Mary, the Princess Royal at the time, was also the Commander-in-Chief of the Royal Scots.

In response to the LNER streamlined expresses, the LMS produced a blueprint for a six-hour non-stop service from London to Glasgow but needed to carry out a trial run to see if it was practical. It was decided to select the senior driver from Crewe North shed, from where locomen worked south to London and north to Perth. Accordingly, Tom Clark was chosen, with fireman Charles Fleet and passed fireman Albert Shaw assisting. The test train from Euston to Glasgow Central was designated 703, and Princess Royal 4-6-2 No 6201 *Princess Elizabeth* was chosen to pull it.

Clark and his crew, the '5A Three' went to London the night before the special runs, lodging with other engine men in the noisy and not select in any way railwaymen's 'barracks' at Camden shed.

On 16 November 1936, Clark and his crew drove the train from London to Glasgow in 5 hours 53 minutes 38 seconds. That in itself was a breathtaking feat, but there was none of the luxury and comforts which a celebrity today might expect: their reward was a night in the 'barracks' at Polmadie shed mucking in with every other locoman.

The following day they made the return journey in 5 hours 44 minutes 14 seconds. Glasgow to London non-stop had been achieved at an average speed of 69 mph, with an average load of 240 tons, a truly outstanding achievement

Crewe's immortal steam legacy: Thirties record-breaker Princess Royal 4-6-2 No 6021 Princess Elizabeth *at Crewe with a preservation era special.* (Brian Sharpe)

for the time, and the footplate crew instantly were feted as national heroes. On arrival at Euston, the trio were taken to Broadcasting House and interviewed by the BBC.

The newspapers of the day ran front page headlines proclaiming '401 Miles Non Stop', 'Railway Ambition Achieved', and 'London-Glasgow Under 6 Hours'. The result of the 802.8-mile round trip shook the railway industry to its roots, as the LMS and Driver Clark had set a new standard. Stanier and the LMS directors knew that they had made the right decision with their plans for the soon-to-be-unveiled 'Coronation Scot' service.

Hornby, the Liverpool manufacturer of model railways, produced an O gauge model of No 6201 as a result. As a promotional exercise, when it was launched on 1 May 1937, Hornby arranged for a photograph to be staged at Edge Hill depot, Liverpool with two schoolboys holding a model alongside the full size locomotive, with Clark and Fleet. Clark was reported as having said. 'It's grand,' a well-known Crewe phrase of the day.

However, for the '5A Three', the record run was just another working day, and the next shift it was business as usual. For a locoman, it was a case of getting up at 2.30 am, cycling to the engine shed and then lighting a fire inside a steam engine, coaxing it into life for a start maybe five hours later. Diesel and electric drivers never had it so good: all they had to do was turn a key, as with a motor car. We may well romanticise about the 'good old days' of the steam era, but many were the old engine hands who were glad when they were over.

Faced with toughening competition from the LNER and its all-conquering A4s, Stanier produced the first of the new streamlined Princess Coronation class Pacifics, No 6220 *Coronation*. In 1937, the LMS chose Tom Clark to drive it and reclaim the world steam locomotive speed record.

The Coronations were an enlarged version of the Princess Royals and at 3300 hp, were the most powerful passenger steam locomotives ever built for the British railway network. A total of 38 were turned out, and many, including this author, regard them as Crewe's finest. They matched the A4s in every respect.

The first five locomotives, Nos 6220–4, were streamlined in a distinctive bulbous air-smoothed casing and painted Caledonian Railway blue with silver horizontal lines to match the 'Coronation Scot' train that they were intended to haul. The streamlining, though certainly eye catching, is widely regarded to have been installed more for publicity purposes than to improve speed. It was said to be of no value at speeds below 90 mph. Indeed, Stanier believed that the added weight and difficulty in maintenance because of the streamlined casing, a permanent source of irritation to locoshed staff, was not offset by any benefits gained at high speed.

Crewe's finest hour? Streamlined Princess Coronation 4-6-2 No 6229 Duchess of Hamilton at speed on an express train in 1938. (National Railway Museum)

The 'Coronation Scot' train on exhibition in January 1939 before its shipment to America. (National Railway Museum)

A streamlined Princess Coronation Pacific pulls into Crewe station in 1938.
(National Railway Museum)

The Coronation class tenders were equipped with a steam-operated coal pusher to bring the coal down to the firing plate, helping firemen to meet the high demands for power during the non-stop run of 299 miles from Euston to Carlisle on the 'Royal Scot' to and from Glasgow Central.

Tuesday, 29 June 1937 saw Tom Clark reach Euston from Crewe, a distance of 158 miles, in 2 hours 9 minutes 45 seconds, with the press trip preceding the launch of the 'Coronation Scot' on 5 July. He made it back to Crewe in 1 hour 59 minutes and reclaimed the record with a top speed of 114 mph, just south of the town.

Again, it was the stuff of legend, and also broken cups and saucers. While the LMS had modified around 50 parts of the London-Glasgow route, realigning track to allow speeds of up to 90 mph on curves, with a minimum of 75 mph, and adapted junctions to enable faster main-line traffic, there were still some areas where restrictions applied. One of these was the 20 mph limit at Crewe.

Clark did not allow sufficient braking distance before entering a series of crossover points on the approach to Crewe, nor did he slow down to anything

What lies beneath the casing of a streamlined Princess Coronation locomotive: the front doors of No 6229 Duchess of Hamilton *are wide open on 15 May 1937 at Crewe.* (National Railway Museum)

like the speed limit. He took the 20 mph reverse curve at around 50 mph, and showed that both the engine and track could handle it. That had much to do with the design of the Coronations, and in particular the leading bogie, rather than derring-do luck. Stanier's assistant Robert Riddles, who was on board the locomotive at the time, recalled that the train was doing 60-70 mph when it approached the Crewe platform signal. The crockery in the dining car came crashing down before Clark slowed to 52 mph on the curve. He recalled: 'With the engine riding like the great lady she is there wasn't a thing we could do about it but hold on and let her take it.' Nonetheless, Clark brought the train to a standstill at Crewe, the locomotive and carriages still on the track.

The speed was such that the final 10½ miles from Whitmore to Crewe had been achieved in slightly under seven minutes. The overall time was 129.75 minutes at an average speed of 73.1 mph, with the final 1.1 miles to Crewe station achieved in 1 minute 19 seconds!

Princess Royal Class 4-6-2 No 6204 Princess Louise. (Author's Collection)

LMS vice-president Sir Ernest Lemon told the guests at the press lunch: 'Of course, gentlemen, you realise that we shan't need to do this kind of thing on every trip of the 'Coronation Scot'; we were coming in a little faster than we shall have to, in the ordinary course.'

The return trip from Crewe back to London was covered in 119 minutes, an average of 79.7 mph, making it one of the fastest ever recorded in Britain. The highlight was the 69.9 miles from Walton to Willesden Junction, which took 47 minutes 1 second at an average of 89.3 mph, with a maximum speed of 100 mph at Castlethorpe water troughs. The net result was that the LMS could claim the fastest start-to-stop runs of over 100 and 150 miles.

The crockery incident led to the LMS and LNER reaching an agreement to halt further dangerous record-breaking runs for the sake of publicity.

The second five locomotives of the class, Nos 6225–6229, were also streamlined, but were painted in the more traditional crimson lake, with gilt horizontal lining. The next batch of Princess Coronation Pacifics was built without streamlining. Smoke deflectors were added from 1945 due to drifting smoke obscuring the crew's forward vision; the last five locomotives were completed with smoke deflectors fitted. Those members of the class which were built with streamlined casings had them removed between 1946 and 1949.

A fortnight after the run with *Coronation*, on 12 July 1937, Clark was chosen to drive the Royal Train from Crewe to Euston, with King George VI, Queen

Elizabeth, Princess Elizabeth and Princess Margaret on board. At Euston, the King summoned Tom from the footplate, an epitome of the typical Crewe locoman, with blackened face and wearing his overalls, and awarded him the Order of the British Empire, for his record runs to and from Glasgow in 1936. It was one of the finest moments of all time for Cheshire and its great steam tradition.

Tom Clark retired to his home town in 1938 and, out of the national limelight, spent his time fishing and playing snooker. He died after a short illness in January 1954, aged 80. He was also presented with a clock by the LMS and it was passed down to other members of the family but, sadly, it was sold during hard times. In modern times, Clark was remembered by the naming of two locomotives in his honour – Class 47 diesel Nos. 47832 and Class 90 electric locomotive No 90014.

The LNER regained the world speed record on 3 July 1938 when A3 No 4468 *Mallard* reached 126 mph while running downhill on Stoke Bank in Lincolnshire.

The streamlined 'Coronation Scot' luxury train inaugurated for the coronation of King George VI, was launched on 5 July 1937 and its six-and-a-half-hour journey time was a huge success. The trains, made up of existing coaches also painted in Caledonian Railway blue to match the new locomotives

Stanier 'Crab' 2-6-0 No 42972 pictured at Crewe in May 1952.
(Frank Ashley/Midland Railway Trust)

Jubilee class 4-6-0 No 45686 St Vincent *at Crewe in November 1950.*
(Frank Ashley/Midland Railway Trust)

rather than the normal LMS crimson lake, left Euston and Glasgow Central simultaneously at 1.30 pm on weekdays and were timed to reach their destinations at 8 pm, stopping at Carlisle to change crews and to pick up and set down passengers to and from London only. It is widely held that its success was largely due to the lessons learned from both No 6201 *Princess Elizabeth* and driver Clark.

The 'Coronation Scot' lasted in service until the outbreak of war in 1939. After the previously-mentioned trip to the USA, when locomotive No 6220 (6229) returned to Britain, the train remained behind and doubled up as living quarters for US Army Quartermaster Corps at Jefferson in Indiana.

Incidentally, the Princess Royal class subsequently became known as 'Lizzies' amongst railwaymen, a name that gathered momentum when the real Princess Elizabeth became Queen in 1952.

Stanier was knighted on 9 February 1943 and became a Fellow of the Royal Society when he retired the following year, after working as a wartime consultant for the Ministry of Supply. The magnitude of that honour was evidenced by the fact that he was the only railway engineer other than George Stephenson to be honoured in this way. He was also elected President of the Institution of Mechanical Engineers for 1944. Stanier died at his home in Rickmansworth in 1965.

8

CHESHIRE RAILWAYS AT WAR

During both world wars, Britain's railway companies were taken into state control under the Railway Executive Committee. The first time round, it ran the railways from 1914 to 1921, after which many of them, especially the smaller concerns, were visibly suffering from lack of maintenance due to austerity measures.

Across the country, civilian passenger services were curtailed, and some were withdrawn, but still traffic increased. Road traffic was virtually suspended and the railways had to cater for a hugely increased workload, in particular the movement of troop trains and military equipment.

The government looked to the railway sector not just to provide transport but also staff to fill up the ranks of the forces, as well as engines for overseas operations. During 1914–18, 184,475 men, or 49%, of the nation's railway staff of military age and over 600 locomotives were taken; large quantities of equipment, including shells and fuses, were manufactured in railway works. In the ticket clerk's office at Chester station is a roll of honour listing GWR employees who perished in the First World War.

Women had to take the place of men in performing engineering tasks. When Crewe began producing munitions in 1915, women workers filled the void in the workforce. One minor change that the war imposed on Crewe Works was that of toilet facilities. In the early days, there were no lavatories; just buses outside the workshops. Eventually, however, common sense and sanitary sanity prevailed and basic toilets were built inside the works. While these had proper flush lavatories, they were intended to be as uncomfortable as possible so that a man had to be desperate to down tools and use them. At first there were two rows of these lavatories back-to-back, and later, begrudgingly, a corrugated iron partition was installed behind each to allow minimum privacy – but there were no doors!

Workers who had become disabled through injuries were re-engaged as lavatory assistants, and had the job of booking anyone who stayed in their semi-cubicle for more than five minutes. If you wanted toilet paper, you were handed an old newspaper. There were no washbasins, as bacteria clearly had not been invented then! However, it all had to change forever when women were taken on, and modern facilities were provided.

In the Second World War, as in the previous global conflict, the Railway Executive Committee again took control, relinquishing it only when the Labour government under Clement Attlee nationalised the railways on 1 January 1948.

When war broke out in 1939, petrol was soon rationed, reducing road transport and placing greater demands on the railway system, of which Crewe was a focal point. The government decreed that freight trains and some special trains, such as those for troop movements, were to be given priority, and so it became custom and practice that passenger trains were frequently held up at junctions and outside main stations, often for the best part of an hour. Ironically, many of them were packed with servicemen and women desperate to get home for a brief spell of leave, only to find that when their train pulled into the station, the buses had stopped for the night and taxis were not available, leaving them to walk miles home.

Because of the shortage of railway staff with so many men joining up, a lack of ticket inspectors meant that tickets on many trains were not checked.

At the outbreak of war, many families living in Britain's big cities made arrangements to send their children by train en masse to the

Noticeboard for the Cheshire Lines Committee's ambulance corps.
(Robin Jones)

countryside, where they would hopefully be safe from Nazi bombing raids. It was a huge psychological and emotional upheaval: youngsters who had never been away from their parents before suddenly found themselves with a suitcase, a gas mask, a handwritten identity label stuck to their coat, and accompanied by teachers as guardians, on a packed train to a mysterious destination where they would never have gone before.

Once there, they would be billeted with families prepared to take them in. While some were poorly treated, others loved the change from the dirty, smoky city environment and had the happiest times of their lives. Evacuees were shipped out to rural Cheshire from Liverpool, Birkenhead and Manchester. Railways played the key role in carrying them to safety, and later bringing them back home.

In the first four days of September 1939, nearly 3,000,000 people were transported from British conurbations to the countryside. Within a week, a quarter of the population of Britain would have a new address. Some returned home after a few months: the bombing of British cities did not begin until 1940, after a period of little military activity dubbed the 'Phoney War' which led the population into a false sense of security. Others stayed until 1944, when the threat of air raids had greatly diminished.

Among the children evacuated to the North West, along with those from the conurbations, were youngsters from the Channel Islands, who had been evacuated prior to the Nazi occupation. Around 2,000 alone were billeted with total strangers in Stockport, and many others found temporary homes in Cheshire and Lancashire. The culture shock for them was even greater than for the young city dwellers who had never been into the heart of the country before, and maybe had never seen the sea. Some of the very youngest Channel Islands children were said to have been scared at the sight of a steam train, having never seen one before, as the last passenger railway on the islands, the Jersey Railway, had closed in 1936. In Cheshire, many of them saw black and white cows, as opposed to cream coloured ones, for the first time.

As barbed wire, tank traps and landmines were installed as defensive measures on many of Britain's beaches, children were evacuated and the population was asked if their journeys were really necessary, it is surprising to find that the railway companies, including the LMS, were still actively prompting summer holidays in wartime. The 1940 *Holidays by LMS* guide ran to 684 pages and featured more than 300 resorts. Cheshire railwaymen's families enjoyed free travel to their chosen destination and normally managed a week a year, maybe at Rhyl or Blackpool. However, during the war, because of rationing, they had to take all their own food with them.

The rapid Nazi advance across the Low Countries and into France had been carried out with the aid of parachutists dropped behind battle lines as an advance force. The British government responded with the formation of the Local Defence Volunteers, later the Home Guard. Many Cheshire railwaymen enlisted in the organisation, as well as serving with Air Raid Precautions. On 30 July 1940, the LMS renamed 'Baby Scot' express 4-6-0 No 5543 as *Home Guard*, and around 50,000 of the company's staff joined the 'Dad's Army' organisation.

Following the retreat from Dunkirk, as one of Britain's busiest junctions, Crewe station was especially busy handling troop trains. In the immediate aftermath of their rescue, hundreds of soldiers slept on the town pavements – local residents finding themselves tripping over them as they went about their daily business.

Another new type of railway passenger to be seen in Cheshire at this time was the Land Army girls, some of whom were trained at Reaseheath, an agricultural college near Nantwich, before being despatched to farms all over Britain to do the work of menfolk who had joined up. They scythed fields, plucked chickens, milked cows by hand, rode carthorses – a form of traction

A typical wartime station scene with troops embarking for their next posting.
(Author's Collection)

which was given a second lease of life in everyday society because of petrol rationing – cleaned out stables, clipped the sheep, fed the animals, made cheese and cream in dairies and planted and harvested crops.

The first air raid in Cheshire took place on Crewe, a prime target because of its strategic importance as part of Britain's railway network and infrastructure, on the evening of 29 July 1940.

New regulations were introduced for running trains during air raids. Signalmen were ordered to stop all trains entering an area under red alert and warn the drivers. The headlamp code carried on the front of the engine then had to be changed to one of a single lamp, indicating that the driver had been told. Passenger trains were then allowed to proceed at 15 mph, later increased to 40 mph. However, in autumn 1940, a purple warning system came in whereby railways were told in confidence when raiding bombers were about, but an attack did not seem imminent. Traffic was allowed to run normally under such conditions. In reality, drivers grew to pay little attention to red alert warnings, even when the sirens sounded.

A simple measure taken in a bid to reduce the chances of being hit in a bombing raid was to camouflage buildings, often by painting factory chimneys green, brown and black so that they blended in with surrounding countryside. You would not fool Luftwaffe pilots by trying to pretend the sprawling Crewe Works was really open fields, but its walls along West Street had silhouettes of streets and houses painted on them.

Outside London, Merseyside was the most heavily bombed area of Britain, with the docks of Liverpool, Birkenhead and Bootle taking a nightly pounding due to their crucial importance to the war effort. The ports, which lay at the western end of the transatlantic shipping routes, handled more than 90% of all the war material brought into Britain from abroad, especially after Churchill and Roosevelt signed the lease-lend agreement, with the railways taking it to the required destinations. Cheshire residents would be woken by the distant sound of explosions and watch in awe the red glow on the horizon to the north. The government was anxious not to let the Nazis know the extent of the damage the Luftwaffe caused and so suppressed reports of the bombing, during which more than 4,000 residents died.

The first major air raid on Liverpool took place over three nights beginning on 28 August 1940 when 160 bombers attacked the city. There were 50 bombing raids between then and the end of the year, and after a brief respite, they resumed during the first seven consecutive days of May 1941, beginning with a hit on Wallasey on the Wirral at 10.15 pm on 1 May. Every railway route into Merseyside was blocked at some point during that week, testing LMS resources to breaking point, and half of the docks were disabled within seven days.

There were many acts of bravery by railwaymen on both sides of the Mersey during these days, when age-old rivalries between the LMS and Cheshire Lines Committee were cast aside and trains ran on each other's routes where necessary after bomb damage. In Liverpool's Clubmoor district, ten LMS staff risked all but certain death to shunt an exploding ammunition train. Indeed, many LMS men and women died in air raids while serving the company.

Norman Tunna, a GWR shunter in Birkenhead, was awarded the George Cross in 1941. He was at work in the town's Morpeth Dock when he heard the air raid siren. Ignoring the warning, he carried on marshalling a goods train containing high explosive bombs for the RAF. He made one last inspection of the train before it set off, and found that a wagon containing many 250 lb bombs had been set alight by incendiary bombs. He coolly fetched a bucket of water and was joined by the locomotive crew. As they fetched more water, Tunna ripped off the sheet covering the wagon in a bid to remove the burning incendiaries. However, one of them fell into the wagon between some of the bombs. Undaunted, Tunna climbed into the wagon and managed to remove the incendiary. He then rejoined the locomotive crew in pumping water over the wagon until the bombs cooled to a safe temperature. A humble shunter was, accordingly, feted as a national hero for his death-defying selflessness.

Tunna died in 1970. On 18 November 1982, British Rail named Class 47 No 47471, after him, and in September 2010 a plaque was unveiled at Birkenhead Central station by Merseyrail and railway chaplain Reverend Richard Cook on the 70th anniversary of his heroics.

Merseyside's rail networks were obviously a prime target. The first Birkenhead Park station, which jointly served the Wirral Railway and Mersey Railway routes, was destroyed by a bomb, while Wallasey Village station had to be extensively rebuilt after the war.

In the 1930s, most British signalboxes were still built out of wood rather than brick, and would have been easily destroyed in a bomb blast or incendiary attack. However, in 1938 London Transport began building signalboxes with reinforced roofs and protective steel, and in early 1939 the LMS started replacing particularly vulnerable signalboxes sited on overhead gantries, and bricking up the windows in the lower storey locking rooms. Some signalboxes were provided with brick-built blast walls to protect them.

Air Raid Precautions, an organisation set up as early as 1924 as a response to fears about the future threat from bomber aircraft, and which supplied gas marks and Anderson air raid shelters, helped with the design of blastproof buildings

Crewe North signalbox, one of a pair designed to withstand bomb blasts. It is now part of Crewe Heritage Centre. (Author)

Built like a battleship and deliberately so: Crewe South Junction has 15 inch thick walls and 18 inch reinforced concrete walls designed to withstand bomb blasts. Built in 1940 to replace a 1907-built LNWR signalbox, today it stands derelict. (David A. Ingham/Creative Commons)

including signalboxes. The LMS opened its first operational ARP signalbox at Crewe Coal Yard on 10 December 1939. ARP signalboxes were intended to replace existing signalboxes that controlled such strategic junctions, and also to control new track layouts for wartime factories and military locations.

Two more ARP signalboxes to control the approaches to Crewe were opened in 1940, as part of a massive resignalling scheme for the station. These had 15 inch thick reinforced concrete walls and 18 inch thick reinforced concrete roofs. A direct hit on a Crewe signalbox could paralyse much of the national network, so the new signalbox had to be especially resilient to blast damage. Another classic example stands at Runcorn. These types of signalbox were so robust that years later, after they became redundant, they were found to be difficult to demolish and many were left standing derelict. Cheshire's Dunham Hill No 2 signalbox, for example, closed on 25 November 1951, but remained in place until late 2008.

Crewe North Junction signalbox is preserved as part of Crewe Heritage Centre. The Crewe re-signalling scheme was carried out amidst conditions of tight security and was little known outside the railway industry. It involved the replacement of the intricate system of 274 traditional semaphore signal arms at the northern and southern ends of the passenger station with 72 coloured lights. The two new signalboxes controlled them all.

The days of Crewe existing exclusively as a railway town had ended in 1938 when Rolls-Royce chose it as the site for a shadow factory, that is, one which mirrored an established production plant in an industrial conurbation at risk of bombing, to make engines for wartime aircraft. Its Merlin engines powered fighter aircraft that took part in the Battle of Britain, described by Winston Churchill as 'Britain's finest hour'.

Also heavily disguised to look like an ordinary row of houses, it was a frequent target for the Luftwaffe. On 29 December 1940, a lone German Junkers 88 bomber released two bombs over the Rolls-Royce factory, causing 17 deaths, despite having been tracked by radar from northern France. It was the greatest loss of life in wartime Crewe. When secret documents were released in 1971, it was revealed that no warning was given as it was not a mass raid. The rule was that sirens were not sounded for a lone enemy plane, and in the absence of an official warning, Ack-ack guns were not allowed to fire unless the aircraft was clearly identified as hostile.

This works employed 10,000 people in 1943, with 300 men loaned from the railway works so that aircraft engine production could be stepped up. The total workforce, as might be expected, fell sharply after it changed over to the production of Rolls-Royce and Bentley cars in 1946.

The carriage of freight by railways was never more vital than during the Second World War. LMS 2F 0-6-0 No 8288, a regular performer on coal trains, stands outside Crewe North shed. (Jarvis Collection/Midland Railway Trust)

During wartime, many railway workshops not only turned out locomotives and stock for the war effort, but also large quantities of military equipment, including shells and fuses. Crewe employed 20,000 people during the Second World War, including an army of women who took over many engineering jobs which were normally the domain of men, who had joined the forces, and produced 150 Covenanter tanks for the army. These were, however, by no means anywhere like as successful as Crewe's finest locomotives, such as the Princess Coronation 4-6-2s, which had their streamlined casings painted black during the war as an austerity measure intended to reduce maintenance.

In 1938, the War Office asked for a new, better armoured cruiser tank to replace the Cruiser IV, and chose the Covenanter. Design work was undertaken by the LMS, and the first 100 were ordered before a single prototype was produced, such was the urgency. In 1941, Crewe had been ordered to build four Covenanters a week, while repairing 40 steam engines. The first Covenanters were not ready until after Dunkirk, and the lack of a test model soon highlighted design flaws which were ironed out in later tank models. By late 1943 the

IS YOUR JOURNEY REALLY NECESSARY?

TICKETS

DON'T HELP HITLER BY TRAVELLING THIS SUMMER!

RAILWAY EXECUTIVE COMMITTEE

A Second World War poster asking people not to travel unless they really had to, thereby leaving space for military personnel. Despite such requests, many resorts thrived during the war, and no doubt Crewe had more than its fair share of holidaymakers passing through. (Author's Collection)

Covenanter was considered too weakly armed and armoured to deal with new German tanks and so was declared obsolete and almost all vehicles scrapped. Only a few ever saw service outside the British mainland.

Meanwhile, the increased workload at Crewe Works was being felt. Ageing engines dating from Victorian times such as Webb's 0-6-0 freight locomotives and the Cauliflowers were not scrapped, as had been the case in the 1930s, but patched up and returned to main line service, such was the need for wartime motive power at all costs.

Elsewhere, purpose-built munitions plants sprang up alongside railways. Royal Ordnance Factory No 13 at Radway Green in Alsager was established in 1940 to make .303 ammunition and within two years employed more than 15,000 people, mostly women, working three shifts per day. By 1945, it was the only factory of its kind to have ammunition-filling capabilities, making it the only fully integrated ammunition producer in Britain.

After the war, the workforce was cut to 1,500 people and production greatly diversified, with domestic cookers and later coins for the Royal Mint being made. One key part of wartime production was the creation of decoy sites, where 'mock' factories were set up to dupe Luftwaffe crews into hitting a harmless target instead of a real one. A decoy for Crewe station, its junction and works was created at Hack Green in the midst of peaceful Cheshire farmland.

The Stanier 8F 2-8-0 heavy freight engine is widely regarded as 'the locomotive that won World War Two'. Built at Crewe in 1942, No 48151 is now owned by the West Coast Railway Company at Carnforth and has regularly run rail tours on the main line. (Author)

Its phoney role in the conflict would not last long, for in 1941 it became RAF Hack Green, a fixed radar installation designed to protect the region between Birmingham and Liverpool from hostile attack. It later played a major role in the Cold War early warning defence system.

Cheshire's railways did not only carry troops, evacuees, raw materials for the war effort and military hardware. They also carried another import – in the form of prisoners of war. There were eleven POW camps in Cheshire.

During the war, Crewe Alexandra FC, the Railwaymen, had a guest player in none other than the legendary England international, Stanley Matthews. The domestic league championship was suspended during the conflict but eventually clubs were allowed to stage games against whatever clubs could muster up teams, including guest players.

Celebrations were held all over Cheshire to mark VE Day on 8 May 1945, with the Square in Crewe being a major centrepiece of festivities involving railwaymen and their families too many and ebullient to count, and again on VJ Day, 15 August that year. Britain with the help of Cheshire's railways had won the day, but the steam age would never be the same again.

9

THE STANDARD ERA – STEAM'S INDIAN SUMMER

After the Second World War, as with the First World War, a maintenance backlog on Britain's railways combined with a lack of long-term investment meant that the system was in places at breaking point and facing a dire financial crisis. Nonetheless, the advantages of running the country's railway companies as one were seized upon by Clement Attlee's Labour government which came to power with a landslide victory in 1945. For both practical and ideological reasons, the new government decided to nationalise the railway sector, and from 1 January 1948, under the British Transport Commission, it became British Railways.

Britain had invented the steam locomotive and Crewe Works had turned out many world-beating types. However, after the cessation of hostilities, Britain was lagging well behind other countries in terms of modernising their railway networks. Before the war, other European countries and the United States had been introducing diesel and electric traction, but Britain was still rooted firmly in the steam age. Admittedly the LMS had produced its first diesel shunter in 1931, and in December 1947, the month before nationalisation, unveiled Britain's first main line diesel locomotive, also built at Derby.

While steam locomotives are labour intensive regarding maintenance and operation, diesels need much less time and labour to operate and maintain. A fire has to be built in a steam locomotive firebox several hours before it runs: a diesel is not dissimilar from a car, which just needs the turning of an ignition key. Also, while electrification of railway lines by providing overhead masts has a high capital outlay, the operating costs are much lower.

Royal Scot No 46148 The Manchester Regiment, *Patriot No 45523* Bangor *and Royal Scot No 46143* The South Staffordshire Regiment *line up outside the Crewe paint shop in British Railways days.* (Frank Ashley/Midland Railway Trust)

Canadian Pacific ordered its first diesel in 1937, turned out its last new steam locomotive in 1949 and completed dieselisation by 1960. The Irish Republic, which had remained neutral in the war, introduced main line diesel railcars in 1950. Of course, those in power in Britain in the late Forties saw that mass dieselisation and electrification of the railways as inevitable, but any large-scale programme at that time would have been a huge leap of faith, trying to run ahead when the national network was still strapped for cash and struggling to get back on its feet. So it was decided that for the present, steam would stay supreme, and British Railways turned to a man who had begun his railway career as a Crewe apprentice in 1909 to head their initial locomotive building policy.

Robert Riddles was born in 1892 and completed his premium apprenticeship at the LNWR in 1913. His mind was not closed to the replacement of steam: while attending Mechanics Institute classes in Crewe, he studied electrical engineering, believing that there would be a future for electric traction. After being badly wounded while serving with the Royal Engineers in France during the First World War, he returned to Crewe Works and was handed responsibility for building a new erecting shop. After studying the Lancashire & Yorkshire Railway's production methods at Horwich Works, he played a sizeable role in the reorganisation of Crewe Works in 1925-27, and afterwards at Derby Works. In 1933 he was appointed as Locomotive Assistant to Stanier at Euston, and in

LNER 0-6-0 No 5194 heads a local passenger train near Knutsford on the rarely photographed Cheshire Lines Committee route on 26 February 1948, shortly after nationalisation. The exposed cab reveals a footplate crew somewhat bemused to find themselves being photographed. (J.F. Russell-Smith/National Railway Museum)

1935 graduated to become his Principal Assistant. When Princess Coronation 4-6-2 No 6229 *Duchess of Hamilton*, masqueraded as No 6220 *Coronation* on a tour of North American in 1939, Riddles drove it for most of the tour, after the designated driver became ill. During the Second World War he served as the Ministry of Supply's Director of Transportation Equipment and designed the War Department's Austerity 2-8-0 and 2-10-0 locomotives. He became vice-president of the LMS in 1944.

At nationalisation, Riddles was appointed a Member of the Railway Executive for Mechanical and Electrical Engineering and in 1948, effectively in the old post of Chief Mechanical Engineer, he stuck with steam. Before he retired in 1953, he oversaw the final period of main line steam locomotive building in Britain, in the form of the twelve British Railways Standard classes.

While British Railways continued to build locomotives to old 'Big Four' designs as an interim measure – in 1948, Crewe was building its final two Princess Coronation Pacifics and was well into constructing a batch of 50 'Black Five' 4-6-0s – steam production nationwide eventually switched over to the Standards, and a total of 999 were built before production ceased in 1960.

The Standards drew largely from LMS designs, but incorporated some features from the other 'Big Four' companies' locomotives. They ranged in size from mighty express passenger locomotives down to tank engines for branch line work, and Crewe was chosen to build the biggest. With the Standards, the glamour of the Thirties – when the LMS competed with the LNER using streamlined Pacifics to see who could reach Scotland from London in the quickest time – was gone. Rivalry, image and prestige were no longer primary concerns. Unlike the designs of their Victorian successors and the magnificent Crewe products of the Thirties, the Standards could not be considered beautiful.

However, they represented the ultimate development of the steam locomotive in Britain. Admittedly they showed no advance in power over the designs of the 'Big Four' companies – they were tailor-made to the economic and social conditions of the post-war years of austerity, and in this criteria, also became true classics in their own right. There was a need for locomotives which were economical to run regardless of the quality of available coal.

Also, the expectation of working conditions had risen. Steam locomotives are by their nature dirty and grimy machines to overhaul, and many older types were not designed with ease of access to individual parts in mind, often in the primitive surroundings of works and engine sheds. If sufficient numbers of men were to be recruited to work on servicing and repairing engines in a post-war world where many other and more lucrative jobs were available, the task had to be made less unattractive, and comparative ease of maintenance was also a factor built into Riddles' Standard designs.

The first Standard to appear was Pacific No 70000 *Britannia*, which emerged from Crewe Works in 1951, the year of the Festival of Britain. It was renowned railway photographer, the late Bishop of Wakefield Eric Treacy, who came up with the name Britannia; many members of the class were named after great Britons and it gave its name to the rest of the class. After successfully undergoing test running on the West Coast Main Line north of Crewe, it was officially named by Transport Minister Alfred Barnes on 30 January 1951.

The Britannias, which had been designed at Derby, were Riddles' response to the Railway Executive for a new express passenger Pacific locomotive, designed specifically to reduce maintenance and using the latest available innovations in steam technology from both Britain and abroad. He came up with a simple,

The first of the British Railways Standards, No 70000 Britannia, *seen leaving Crewe station with a heritage era special.* (Brian Sharpe)

standard and efficient design, able to match the power of the LMS Pacifics that went before, but lacking their razzamatazz. Their 6ft 2in driving wheels facilitated sustained fast running with heavy passenger trains, yet were small enough to allow them be used for goods trains. The initial order was for 25 locomotives, but such was the demand for the Britannias on the Eastern Region that the class total of 55 were constructed over three batches at Crewe Works.

The Britannias proved to be popular engines with crews in most of the British Railways regions, but the Western Region, the successor to the GWR, disliked them to the point of declaring them surplus to requirements at two major sheds, partially due to old rivalries such as that which had existed in Cheshire with the LMS, and a preference for GWR-designed engines. You might nationalise the railways into one entity, but you could never erode the great pride that railwaymen felt for their employers in the days of steam, not least of all the men of Crewe.

As well as building all the Britannias between 1951 and 1954, Crewe constructed the ten smaller but similar Standard 6 or Clan Pacifics between December 1951 and the following March. Their smaller boilers were part of

Older designs still held good in the 1950s, the last great decade of steam. LMS Patriot
No 45517 passes Whitmore Troughs while picking up water with an
Up train on 3 August 1957. (Dick Blenkinsop/LMS-Patriot Project)

British Railways Crew-built Clan 4-6-2 No 72005 Clan Macgregor passed
Chester 3A signalbox with a freight working on 29 August 1964.
(Ben Brooksbank/Creative Commons)

weight-saving measures designed to make them suitable to run over more routes than the Britannias. However, reception from locomotive crews was mixed, and after no more were built due to an acute steel shortage in the early Fifties, the class was eventually deemed a failure by British Railways.

Many believe that the BR Standard 9F heavy freight 2-10-0s, which normally hauled huge coal trains but could be pressed into passenger service if required, were the best of the Riddles designs. They were built to last 40 years, and Crewe built 198 out of a total of 251. Indeed, the final steam locomotive built at Crewe was 9F No 92250 in 1958. It was said to be the 7,331st since construction had begun.

The final Standard design of all was that of the unique Class 8P No 71000 *Duke of Gloucester*, which was built at Crewe in 1954, as a direct replacement for Princess Royal 4-6-2 No 46202 *Princess Anne*. The latter had been destroyed in the Harrow & Wealdstone rail disaster on the West Coast Main Line on 8 October 1952, Britain's worst peacetime train accident in which 112 people were killed and a further 10 died afterwards from their injuries.

British Railway's ultimate steam design, No 71000 Duke of Gloucester, *but only one was built before an end to the age of steam was declared.* (Brian Sharpe)

Princess Anne was a rebuild of an earlier unique Crewe product, the LMS Turbomotive No 6202, which used steam turbines instead of conventional cylinders. Designed by Stanier, it was built in 1935, when its innovative design which greatly boosted thermal efficiency was a huge success. It ran for more than 300,000 miles in service before it was withdrawn in 1949. Again, it was the outbreak of war and subsequent austerity measures which prevented the concept from being developed to the point where a production batch might be ordered. After the war ended and Stanier was gone, there was nobody to champion the Turbomotive cause.

It had only been back in service for two months before the Harrow & Wealdstone tragedy, in which it had been one of two engines double heading an express train from Euston to Liverpool and Manchester via Crewe. Taken back to Crewe, it was deemed beyond economical repair and scrapped.

The last steam locomotive built for British Railways, 9F 2-10-0 No 92220, runs a light engine through Northwich en route from Chester to the National Railway Museum at York on 21 May 1983. Crewe built many 9Fs, but this one came from Swindon. (David A. Ingham/Creative Commons)

Electric signalling apparatus inside Crewe North signalbox. (Author)

Riddles had frequently argued for a Standard Class 8 Pacific to be added to the Standard range, but was persistently turned down by the Railway Executive on cost grounds as it was deemed that there were sufficient Class 8 locomotives in service. However, the loss of *Princess Anne* paved the way for another 8P to be built for the heavy expresses which ran through Cheshire, and Riddles seized on the opportunity to win approval for his design to be built, initially as a prototype.

The new design was somewhat revolutionary for Britain as it drew heavily on Italian locomotive practice using a modified form of Caprotti valve gear, allowing precise control of steam admission to the cylinders while improving exhaust flow and boiler draughting. In theory it should have created a superior locomotive, paving the way for a production batch, but there were also basic design flaws which, combined with undetected deviations from the drawings made during construction at Crewe, led to No 71000, being unpopular with its crews and turning in less than impressive results.

Based for its whole working life at Crewe North shed, *Duke of Gloucester* hauled boat trains between Crewe and Holyhead until it was withdrawn in 1962 after only eight years, without having realised its true potential. We will return to its story in Chapter 12.

Wrecked Princess Coronation 4-6-2 No 46251 City of Nottingham *after the Winsford tragedy of 1948.* (Ben Brooksbank/Creative Commons)

Overall, Crewe constructed 289 of the Standards. Despite the excellence of many of their designs, history records that they were just a stop gap, with their days numbered as the UK economy began to recover, and diesel and electric traction queued up to take their place.

As a sad postscript to the glory days of steam, one of the worst rail tragedies in history occurred at Winsford on 17 April 1948, when a soldier on leave pulled the communication cord of the 5.40 pm Glasgow to Euston train and then was seen to get off. The stationary train was then hit by a postal express hauled by Princess Coronation 4-6-2 No 6251 *City of Nottingham* at between 40–45 mph. The signalman at Winsford had wrongly reported the passenger train clear of its section and accepted the postal train. Twenty-four passengers were killed, and the impact was so severe that only five of the ten passenger coaches could be pulled away on their wheels. Winsford was certainly a black spot on the county's railways. At nearby Coppenhall Junction on the evening of Boxing Day 1962, at the start of the big freeze which lasted for several weeks, plummeting temperatures caused points to freeze around Crewe and trains were being held at red signals, including a diesel-hauled Glasgow to Euston train. The driver found the telephone to Coppenhall Junction, the next signalbox ahead, out of order, and decided to proceed to the next signal where there was another telephone. In the blackness he did not see the Liverpool to Birmingham express stationary ahead, and ploughed into it at 20 mph. A total of 18 passengers were killed and 34 injured.

10

ALL CHANGE ...

Life in a steam shed, whether it be the 1830s or the 1960s, would be hard, yet most railwaymen developed a great sense of pride in their job and built up a unique camaraderie with their colleagues.

Many short-trousered schoolboys crowding platforms at Crewe or Chester in the summer holidays yearned to be a train driver, and their ultimate goal on their lineside visits was to be allowed to 'cab' a particular locomotive, maybe a glamorous Princess Royal or Princess Coronation, and stand for a few moments on the footplate. It was akin to getting a backstage pass to meet a modern chart-topping pop star.

Yet an engineman's life was far from glamorous. He would rise in the early hours, when few others were awake, and make his way to the shed, by bicycle or on foot, maybe wearing a long-sleeved flannel vest and ankle-length 'long john' underpants on particularly cold bitter winter mornings.

Before dawn broke, he would be hard at work preparing his engine for the day's duties. He might load coal into the bunker or tender, clear piles of ash from the smokebox, clean the locomotive, or light the fire in the firebox. It would take several hours for the boiler to warm up to the point where a sufficient head of steam would be raised to allow the locomotive to move.

After a long day's work driving or firing the engine, it would be returned to its shed, where the last of the glowing coals had to be thrown out and the engine allowed to go cold, ready for the next day's work. The engineman would have left his home in darkness and returned to it in darkness. Still, very few of them, once they had risen through the ranks from cleaner to driver, a process that could take two to three decades would have exchanged their work for anything else (today's diesel drivers can drive their trains after a six-month course).

With the mighty Standards being turned out at a steady rate from Crewe and

The 1.20 pm Llandudno-Derby summer Saturday express enters Crewe on 19 July 1958, coming off the Chester line across the main lines, and headed by LMS Jubilee 4-6-0 No 45700 Amethyst *piloting Stanier 'Black Five' 4-6-0 No 45026. Notice the masts that are already being erected for the electrification to Manchester 18 months later, and the numerous trainspotters that crowd the end of Platform 4.* (Ben Brooksbank/Creative Commons)

other works, it seemed that this way of dirty, grimy, filthy, backbreaking, call it what you will, way of life would never change. Yet within five years of the appearance of *Britannia*, railwaymen were told that it would soon be all swept away forever. As Britain's financial situation eased, rationing ceased and the austerity years became less austere, British Railways looked to its next stage of development, beyond the Standards.

By the Fifties, road transport presented the biggest challenge to the railway network in its history. Just as the railways had killed off the stagecoaches, so cars, lorries and buses, which offered infinitely greater flexibility and versatility than a form of transport that had to remain on a fixed track, now threatened their survival. British Railways officials knew that services must be made more attractive both to passengers and freight operators, and this would best be done by increasing speed, reliability, safety and line capacity.

On 1 December 1954, the blueprint for the future of the railways was published. The report was known as *Modernisation and Re-Equipment of the British Railways*, or the 1955 Modernisation Plan for short. Its most dramatic measure was to completely eradicate steam locomotives and replace them with diesel and electric alternatives, proposing the electrification of principal main lines, including the Euston to Birmingham/Crewe/Manchester/ Liverpool route. The report also recommended a new fleet of passenger and freight rolling stock, the creation of large goods marshalling yards with automated shunting to streamline freight handling, mass resignalling and track renewal, and the closure of more unprofitable lines and routes which duplicated others. It was proposed to spend £1,240 million over 15 years to achieve these goals.

A government White Paper of 1956 stated that modernisation would help eradicate the railway's growing financial deficit by 1962. However, nobody really knew what was around the corner in the modern age, and other factors would come into play. Historians have said that what hit the railways hardest at this time was not the lack of modern traction or motor transport, but the national rail strike of 1955.

During the 1950s, as the British economy underwent a post-war boom, trade unions found themselves able to demand better wages and working conditions for their members by use of the threat of strike action. Days after Anthony Eden's Conservative government won a General Election victory, the union representing train drivers in Britain, the Associated Society of Locomotive Engineers and Firemen (ASLEF), called a strike over a pay dispute. The union was demanding a pay rise which amounted to around the price of an extra packet of cigarettes a week.

Although locomen who belonged to the National Union of Railwaymen continued to work, the ASLEF strike lasted from 28 May to 14 June, and brought British industry to a standstill. The dispute cost British Railways around £12 million in lost revenue. While a quarter of the normal passenger traffic and a third of the freight was still carried, the strike for what was a miniscule sum of money irreparably damaged the public's regard for train travel. Many ordinary people found that once they had found alternative road transport to get to work and do their shopping, it was more convenient and often cheaper. After the strike was resolved with a compromise solution, there was a switch en masse by both passengers and freight customers from rail to road.

The railways' pick-up goods services were hit particularly hard. In the steam age, most stations had their own goods shed and sidings. Wagons and vans would be loaded or unloaded inside the goods shed, and when the next freight train came along, they would be shunted onto or off it. On branch lines, often the train engine performed the shunting, detaching itself to run into the sidings to fetch the loaded wagons, or to take empty ones into the goods shed. It was a time-consuming exercise, that often required far more work than, say, loading

'Black Five' No 45402 shunts freight wagons at Warrington Bank Quay on 21 September 1966. (Author's Collection)

goods on or off the back of a lorry, and many firms discovered that fact for themselves during the ASLEF strike. Before the Modernisation Plan was published, early diesel multiple units were being introduced on part of the national rail network, replacing steam-hauled trains primarily on branch lines. Indeed, the GWR had introduced diesel railcars in 1933 with enormous success.

The Modernisation Plan sparked off a mass rush to modernise, with several types of diesel locomotive being developed and placed on the production lines before they had really been tested. Some of these types would not even last in service until the end of steam under British Railways.

Crewe began building main line diesels in 1957, with the first of a batch of 135 of Class 08 diesel-electric shunters, an evolution of the pioneer LMS design of the Thirties. In 1959, it started work on BR/Sulzer Type 2 diesel electric locomotives, later known as Class 24.

However, by the end of the 1950s, it was obvious that the hurried implementation of the Modernisation Plan was not clawing back the promised £85 million a year from the British Railway deficit. With the ASLEF strike fresh in its mind, the government was determined not to let the country be held to ransom again, and switched its transport policy from rail to road. There was a growing feeling in the corridors of power that railways were an expensive and increasingly outmoded legacy from Victorian times, which were being propped

It is now widely accepted that the age of steam came to an end too soon. Several diesel types were rushed into production in the late Fifties without being properly tested, such as the 20 Class 28 Metropolitan Vickers Co-Bos. All but one were scrapped by 1969, only months after British Railways ended steam services. The lone survivor, D5705, now preserved, is seen inside Crewe Works during an open day in 2005. (Author)

up with vast amounts of taxpayers' money when roads were being built to do the same job more effectively.

Closures of lossmaking railway lines, mainly rural branches, firstly to passengers and later to freight, had begun in the 1930s, but gathered pace in the Fifties. Across the country, British Railways closed 925 route miles between 1953 and 1958. Among these early Cheshire casualties were passenger services on the North Staffordshire Railway route from Harecastle (Kidsgrove) to Wheelock & Sandbach on 28 July 1930; the LNWR route from Tattenhall Junction on the Crewe-Chester line to Malpas and Whitchurch which closed to passengers on 16 September 1957 and to goods in November 1963; the GWR and LNWR Joint line from Hooton to West Kirkby which lost its passenger trains on 17 September 1956 and freight in 1962. Passenger services were withdrawn from the Middlewich line in 1960 and Stockport-Warrington two years later.

The October 1959 General Election saw the appointment of Ernest Marples as Minister of Transport, where his first move was to impose tighter control over the British Transport Commission and call a halt to the excesses of the modernisation programme.

An independent advisory panel chaired by industrialist Sir Ivan Stedeford was set up to investigate the structure and finances of the British Transport Commission. Among its members was Dr Richard Beeching, a physicist and engineer at Imperial Chemical Industries (ICI). Following the panel's recommendations, Marples presented a White Paper to the House of Commons in December 1960, calling for the splitting of the BTC into smaller bodies, including a new British Railways Board. It also set financial targets for the railways, which would lead to cuts.

The Select Committee of the House of Commons on Nationalised Industries decided that the British Transport Commission should make its decisions exclusively on considerations of 'direct profitability'. The Transport Act 1962 broke up the BTC as recommended. Ominously, it also introduced new legislation for the closure of railway lines.

Despite briefly rallying at the end of the Fifties, British Railways' annual loss on operating account reached nearly £87 million in 1961. That was in a time when only one in nine families owned a car: with car and motorbike ownership rates soaring, what would be the future for railways?

On 15 March that year, Marples told Parliament that Beeching was to be appointed as British Railways chairman as from 1 June. His brief was simple: cut the deficit. No longer would there be a special case for the railways: they would have to compete in a free market in the same way as any other business, without the continuing vast subsidies.

During the week ending 23 April 1962, a study commissioned by Beeching found that 30% of route miles carried just one per cent of passengers and freight, and half of all stations contributed just two per cent of income. Half the total route mileage carried about four per cent of the total passenger miles, and around five per cent of the freight ton miles; revenue from them amounting to £20 million with the costs double that figure. From the least-used 50% of stations, the gross revenue from all traffic did not even cover the cost of the stations themselves. On branch lines, data showed it was doubtful if the revenue from up to 6,000 passengers a week covered train movement costs alone. The writing for many routes and services was now on the wall.

The big shock came on 27 March 1963, when Beeching's report, *The Reshaping of British Railways,* was published. By then, it was little more than old railwaymen had anticipated, having seen traffic all but disappear on many routes which they knew were doomed to closure. However, even they greeted the full extent of the proposed closures in the report, called the Beeching Axe by the press, with utter horror.

Out of around 18,000 miles nationwide, 5,000 which mainly comprised cross-country routes and rural branches, should close completely over a seven-year period, it said. Some lines would close altogether, while others would lose their passenger services and be kept open for freight. Elsewhere, intermediate stations on main lines would be closed to save money and speed up trains between the major destinations. The report also confirmed the closures of routes recommended for withdrawal of services before it was published.

Amongst the Cheshire lines listed were the whole of the Cheshire Lines Committee routes west of Chester, Chester General to Liverpool Lime Street, Glazebrook-Stockport Tiviot Dale, Hayfield/Macclesfield-Romiley-Manchester

Cheshire railwaymen were amongst those who marched through Manchester on 13 October 1963 in protest against the Beeching cuts, but largely in vain. (National Railway Museum)

Piccadilly, St Helens Shaw Street-Earlestown-Warrington Bank Quay and New Brighton-Chester Northgate-Wrexham Central (local services).

Services with intermediate stations withdrawn included Carlisle-Preston-Warrington-Crewe, Chester General-Crewe, Chester General-Warrington Bank Quay-Manchester Exchange, Crewe-Shrewsbury and Stalybridge-Stockport Edgeley.

The report also confirmed the closure of the Crewe-Wellington route which had been previously recommended, with Wellington to Nantwich services being axed in September 1963, just a few months after Beeching dropped his bombshell.

Hundreds of poorly-used station goods yards were to be axed, spelling the end for the pick-up goods service in Cheshire. Freight services were far more harshly hit than passenger trains in the Beeching report. Liner trains which had the

Hadlow Road station was opened on 1 October 1866 as part of the GWR and LNWR Joint Railway's Hooton to Parkgate branch line. It closed to passengers in 1956, well before Beeching. The trackbed of the Hooton-West Kirby branch was selected in 1968 to create Britain's first country park, the Wirral Country Park, opening in 1973. The park forms the central section of Wirral Way, a 120-mile cycleway and footpath that follows the course of the railway between West Kirby and Hooton. The station building and the eastbound platform were restored to their 1950s condition, serving as a Wirral Way visitor centre.
(Chrispd1975/Creative Commons)

benefit of economies of scale were to be introduced where possible to replace wagonload freight, but by and large this did not materialise. However, Crewe lost its marshalling function to Warrington in 1972 as a result.

Although Beeching's recommendations in Cheshire were largely enacted, several threatened intermediate stations such as Broadbottom, Frodsham, Helsby and Newton (for Hyde) survived, while the Chester-Runcorn-Liverpool service lasted until 1975. Beeching's report angered many, and he has been described as the most hated civil servant in Britain of all time, the man who took away our railways and scrapped our steam engines, replacing them with soulless blue-and-white boxes with motors inside. His recommendations generated much bitterness amongst railwaymen, who saw their world snatched away, leaving them on the scrap heap, often after several generations.

Yet others see him as a champion of the railway, merely streamlining the process of inevitable closures that had been underway for many years, and pruning the network to the point where it could survive in an age dominated by road transport. With the rising numbers of passenger journeys reported on the UK network in recent years, there is evidence to suggest that in many ways, he may have been right.

Beeching was bitterly attacked by Labour politicians before they won the 1964 General Election. Afterwards, despite all the pre-election promises to stop them, Beeching's cuts were not only implemented, but even more closures were introduced by Labour, who kept him in place. For instance, the Great Central Railway's Woodhead route from Manchester through the north-easternmost corner of Cheshire to Sheffield, which had been electrified and reopened amidst a blaze of national publicity in 1955 portraying it as the gleaming future of the nation's railways, was closed to passenger services from 5 January 1970, in favour of the alternative route between the two cities through the Hope Valley, because of social considerations. Beeching had certainly not called for the closure: indeed, he saw the Woodhead route as part of his blueprint for future development of the railways. Indeed, he became the ultimate bogey man: many people including the local press still make the mistake of referring to a particular line as being a 'Beeching closure' despite historical facts showing it was shut before or after his time.

The mass closures of the Sixties saw many local people protest to save their services. A local Transport Users Consultative Committee had the power to hear public objections, and make appropriate recommendations to the Minister of Transport, who in a few cases overruled Beeching's recommendation and kept some lines and stations open. Once the appeal process was exhausted, statutory closure notices would be posted.

The final day of services often saw trains packed out, with enthusiast specials with special headboards being run, behind steam where possible. The late Fifties and early Sixties saw more local steam services being replaced by diesel multiple units, which themselves had to be transferred elsewhere once the branch on which they ran closed. DMUs had been brought in to cut the cost of running branch lines using steam locomotives, and were generally welcomed by the public, but even such measures could not stem many of the colossal losses that were being made.

Tracks were ripped up sometimes within a few days of the last trains being run, leaving empty station buildings to the mercy of vandals, Mother Nature and the elements. Around the country, withdrawn steam locomotives were taken to scrapyards where often within a few days they were reduced to a pile of metal by the cutter's torch. As Bob Dylan said, the times they were a-changing.

The end of steam, however, brought vast improvements to Cheshire's trunk route, the West Coast Main Line, which had been selected in 1955 for electrification. The 25kV overhead electrification between Euston and Glasgow was completed in stages between 1959 and 1974: the first length, Crewe-Manchester, finished on 12 September 1960, followed by Crewe-Liverpool on 1 January 1962. The first electric trains from London ran on 12 November 1965.

Once electrification was complete between London and the North West, new high-speed long-distance services were introduced in 1966, launching British Rail's highly successful Inter-City brand, bringing unprecedented journey times such as London to Manchester or Liverpool down to 2 hours 30 minutes for the twice-daily Manchester Pullman.

We often look wistfully back at the demise of steam with some regret: however, at the time, familiarity with steam had bred contempt, and the public loved the new blue-and-white electric locomotives and the comfort their trains promised. Preparing for the launch of electric services from London to Liverpool and Manchester, British Rail produced souvenir items as part of a publicity drive. Within a few weeks of going on sale, almost the entire stock of 50,000 penny blue and white 'London Midland Express' lapel badges were sold. Shoulder travel bags bearing the legend 'Inter-City Electric' and sold at main stations for 15 shillings also proved popular.

Some steam locomotive types were permitted to continue running on the electrified route through Cheshire, but carried a warning symbol on the side of the cab to let shed staff know that they complied with height clearances and would not come into contact with the overhead cables.

With the opening of the new electrified West Coast Main Line, it was curtains for the GWR route to Birkenhead. Beeching found that Birkenhead Woodside

The GWR's Birkenhead Woodside station in 1961: it became a classic Beeching closure. (Ben Brooksbank/Creative Commons)

station was surplus to requirements, as most of the routes served could also be taken from Liverpool Lime Street.

In March 1967, the last steam locomotive ran out of the station as services to Birmingham were withdrawn and the route was curtailed north of Wolverhampton, leaving the hourly diesel service to Chester and trains to Helsby. These were subsequently terminated at Rock Ferry, and Birkenhead Woodside closed to passengers on 5 November 1967, being demolished two years later.

Despite local protests, Chester lost its Northgate station as a result of the Beeching cuts. Chester Northgate goods station closed on 5 April 1965, and passenger services from Chester Northgate to New Brighton and Wrexham were withdrawn on 9 September 1968, leaving only an hourly DMU service to Manchester to use the large Cheshire Lines Committee terminus. So a connection was laid between the CLC line and the Birkenhead Joint Line at Mickle Trafford to allow the Manchester trains to be diverted to Chester General, and the complete closure of Chester Northgate on 6 October 1969. The site is now a leisure centre called Northgate Arena.

After the building of new steam locomotives ceased at Crewe, the works continued to carry out repairs to them until 2 February 1967 when Britannia Pacific No 70013 *Oliver Cromwell* left after being serviced. It found fame as one of the four locomotives that hauled the last steam passenger train on British Railways, the 'Fifteen Guinea Special' enthusiast tour from Liverpool Lime Street via Manchester to Carlisle and back on 11 August 1968.

CHESHIRE'S MINIATURE STEAM REVOLUTION

We have seen how one of the biggest railway works in the world sprang up in Cheshire to serve one of Britain's two busiest trunk routes, the West Coast Main Line. However, the county also saw the start of another form of steam railway revolution, but on a much smaller scale – literally.

Miniature railways have been a popular feature of many traditional British seaside resorts for a century or more, offering rides to youngsters of all ages, often along a circuit of track, and they can also be found at many destinations inland, such as theme parks, zoos and stately homes.

Many such lines are built to 15 inch gauge, a sort of 'halfway house' between large model railways capable of carrying passengers and 'true' narrow gauge – and only 3 inches narrower than the internal railway steam at Crewe Works!

It was Sir Arthur Percival Heywood, 3rd Baronet, who built a 4 inch gauge model railway with a steam locomotive as a teenager. He wanted something that his younger brothers could ride on, and so built a 9 inch gauge line too, but it was too unstable to carry passengers properly. After his marriage in 1872 he set up home at Duffield Bank in Derbyshire and fraternised with many Midland Railway directors who lived locally. Aware of experiments by the Royal Engineers to develop small railways which could be used in warfare, he built a 15 inch gauge line on his land. Known as the Duffield Bank Experimental Railway, it had steep gradients and small radius curves.

While his miniature railway attracted much interest, the only person who commissioned him to build one was the Duke of Westminster. His Eaton Hall

Shelagh at the Eaton Hall terminus of the Eaton Hall Railway. The original saloon carriage shown in the picture was, like the rest of the rolling stock on this little railway, built by Sir Arthur Heywood in his workshops at Duffield Bank near Derby. He delivered it to Cheshire's Eaton Hall Railway in 1904. According to driver Harry Wilde's visitors book from Eaton, Sir Winston Churchill was carried in January 1905 and in the same year so were King Edward VII, Baron Rothschild and the King of Spain. In 1947 it was moved to the Romney, Hythe & Dymchurch Railway but returned to Eaton Hall in 1980. In 2004 a replica was completed by the estate staff at Eaton Hall using ironwork from the original body, which was then donated to the Heywood Collection by the Duke of Westminster and has been restored at the Perrygrove Railway where in August 2007 it was recommissioned by Sir Peter Heywood, great grandson of Sir Arthur. The restoration was carried out by James Waterfield, who has also built a working replica of Eaton Hall locomotive Ursula. (The Heywood Collection)

Railway was also built to 15 inch gauge and ran three miles from his Cheshire stately home to the GWR station sidings at Balderton on the Shrewsbury to Chester line, with a maximum gradient of 1-in-70. With the addition of branch lines, including one serving the estate's brickyard, the total length was expanded to 4½ miles. Amongst its engineering features was a level crossing of the main Wrexham to Chester road.

A replica of the original Heywood locomotive Ursula *at the modern-day
Eaton Hall Railway in 2002, driven by its builder James Waterfield.*
(Michael Crofts/Perrygrove Railway)

Three engines were supplied, the first an 0-4-0T named *Katie*, followed by
two identical 0-6-0Ts named *Shelagh* and *Ursula*. Thirty-four open waggons and
a four-wheeled brake van carried coal, bricks and timber. There was an open 16-
seat bogie coach, a bogie parcel van, a 12-seater closed bogie passenger vehicle
and a bogie brake van seating four inside and four outside. More wagons were
subsequently built by the Eaton Estate and rebuilt over the years.

The Eaton Hall Railway, together with the 15-inch gauge line at Blakesley
Hall in Northamptonshire, effectively provided the blueprint for the hundreds
of seaside, tourist attraction and private railways built in the 20th century,
including the world-famous Romney, Hythe & Dymchurch Railway in Kent,
the Fairbourne Railway in central Wales and the Ravenglass & Eskdale Railway
in the Lake District. All of them owe a debt to the little Cheshire line, and proved
that not only did steam trains pave the way for millions of people to take seaside
holidays, but would also provide popular entertainment during their stay.

A collection of restored original and replica Heywood stock has been set up
at the 15 inch gauge Perrygrove Railway in the Forest of Dean.

12
CHESHIRE STEAM'S SECOND COMING

As we have seen, in 1954 unique Class 8P Pacific No 71000 *Duke of Gloucester* not only became British Railways' last express passenger locomotive, but also its final steam design. Although the emergence of 9F 2-10-0 No 72220 *Evening Star*, the 999th Standard and the last main line steam engine built by British Railways, from Swindon Works, took place six years later, No 71000 brought the curtain down on a design technology that had begun with Richard Trevithick's first steam railway locomotive in 1802.

Duke of Gloucester lasted only eight years in service. A prototype of what had been intended to be a much bigger class, until the 1955 Modernisation Plan called a halt to the steam proceedings, No 71000 incorporated three sets of modified Caprotti valve gear, relatively new to British locomotive engineering and more efficient than Walschaerts or Stephenson valve gear. However, 'the *Duke*' was considered as a failure by locomotive crews due to its poor steaming characteristics and its heavy fuel consumption. There were also problems with poor draughting of the locomotive which led to it running at slow speeds and failing to keep to timetables. Because of the Modernisation Plan, British Railways decided not to proceed with modifications to No 71000 which would have made its design far more successful. It was withdrawn in 1962.

It was initially selected for the National Collection, the list of steam locomotives that were designated for official preservation by the government because of their historic merit. However, the experts who compiled the list subsequently decided that only the cylinder arrangement of No 71000 was of historical interest. So one of the *Duke*'s outside cylinders was removed for display at the Science Museum, while the locomotive was sold off for scrap, to one Dai Woodham, whose breaker's yard was located at Barry in South Wales.

Having been scrapping redundant railway locomotives and rolling stock since

116

The last express passenger steam locomotive built for use by British Railways was one-off Pacific No 71000 Duke of Gloucester *at Crewe in 1954. However, it realised its true potential only after it was preserved, despite being partially cut up, and therefore forms a unique bridge between the golden days of Cheshire steam and the heritage era. It is pictured heading the Railway Touring Company's 'Great Britain' through Magor in South Wales in April 2007.* (Brian Sharpe)

1958, in 1965 Dai worked out that scrapping wagons was more profitable than cutting up steam engines, and left them rusting in long sidings. Eventually, Britain's railway preservation movement, which began with the volunteer-led takeover of the Talyllyn Railway in central Wales in 1951, had developed to the point where 213 of the scrap engines were bought for preservation purposes.

At first, nobody considered No 71000 minus its cylinder to be a feasible restoration project. However, in 1974 a group of enthusiasts bought it under the banner of the Duke of Gloucester Steam Locomotive Trust, and spent 13 years restoring it to running order, at the Great Central Railway in Leicestershire.

Trust members, amazingly, went one big stage further. During the rebuilding of No 71000, they discovered the reason for the design faults that caused its poor performance on the main line, and rectified them. Firstly, the chimney was too small compared with similar locomotives, causing the poor boiler. Secondly, the grate air inlet dampers had not been built in accordance with the drawings, and were too small, resulting in poor air supply and inefficient combustion. Thirdly, the superior Kylchap exhaust system that had been recommended by Crewe engineers was finally installed.

The net result was that when it ran again, *Duke of Gloucester*'s failings had been addressed, and it could finally demonstrate its true potential as a powerful express passenger locomotive. The locomotive returned to its Crewe birthplace in 1987 to be retyred, and on 15 March 1990, made a triumphant return to the main line. The spirit and tradition of Crewe steam engineering lived on! Since then, No 71000 has been a popular performer both on main line steam charters and on heritage railways all over Britain.

Steam engineering at Crewe did not die: events proved that it had merely slept for a few decades. In the late Seventies, former British Rail employee Pete Waterman began making his millions as a record producer, and then as a songwriter as part of the hugely-successful Eighties hit-making trio of Stock, Aitken and Waterman. He decided to invest much of his fortune in his first love, railways.

In 1993, he formed the modern-day London & North Western Railway Co. Ltd. as a direct result of the Conservative government's privatisation of the rail industry. It responded to a demand from the newly-independent train operating companies for convenient and affordable servicing and repair facilities.

The business was located in the Crewe South carriage shed, and very quickly earned a reputation for quality workmanship. However, in addition to servicing main line locomotives and carriages, it also diversified into repairing and overhauling steam locomotives.

In 2005, Pete Waterman split the operation in two, demerging LNWR Heritage Co. Limited which would concentrate on

Pop mogul Pete Waterman sits in the cab of No 70000 Britannia *during an open day at Crewe Works. (Author)*

Pete Waterman's LNWR Works at Crewe is keeping the town's great steam engineering tradition alive today. In 2010, No 70000 Britannia is seen having its boiler lifted back into its frames as part of a major overhaul. (Author)

steam, backed by an apprenticeship scheme. In 2009, LNWR was sold to Arriva Trains, which was subsequently acquired by main line operator DB Schenker, but Waterman retained control of LNWR Heritage.

Pete Waterman, who has received an OBE for his work, said: 'It was just too depressing to us to think that having invented the railway we couldn't sustain an industry that would protect this wonderful legacy and allow future generations to enjoy the spectacle of seeing a steam locomotive (or an early diesel or electric loco) as it was intended – working, not mounted on a plinth and stuck in a museum.' He put his money where his mouth was. One locomotive that he sponsored for restoration to full working order was a Crewe classic, in the form of the National Collection's 19-built LNWR G2a 'Super D' 0-8-0 No 49395.

Thankfully, several masterpieces made by Cheshire craftsmen at Crewe Works are still very much with us today. No 6201 *Princess Elizabeth*, which broke records with driver Tom Clark's hand on the regulator, was bought straight out of British Railways service in 1962 by the Princess Elizabeth Locomotive Society, and regularly hauls special trains on the main line today. Also preserved, by the Princess Royal Class Locomotive Trust, is sister No 46203 *Princess Margaret Rose*.

Three members of Crewe's magnificent Princess Coronation class also survive.

No 6235 (British Railways No 46235) *City of Birmingham*, which was built in 1939, was withdrawn from service in September 1964 and overhauled at Crewe, for preservation as a static exhibit in the Birmingham Museum of Science and Industry, which resisted subsequent proposals to return it to steam on the main line. It is now displayed in Birmingham's modern Thinktank science museum.

A far more glittering afterlife awaited No 6229 *Duchess of Hamilton*, built in 1938 as the tenth member of the class, as a red-liveried streamliner. As previously mentioned, in 1939 it exchanged identities with No 6220 *Coronation* and was sent to the USA along with the 'Coronation Scot' train to star at the 1939 New York World's Fair. The locomotive was shipped back in 1942, and the identities of the pair were exchanged again the following year.

After being painted in wartime black livery in November 1944, No 6229's streamlined casing was removed in December 1947. When the railways were nationalised on 1 January 1948, it became No 46229. It was withdrawn from service in February 1964, but together with sister No 6233 *Duchess of Sutherland* was bought by Sir Billy Butlin, along with other locomotives, for static display at his holiday camps. He knew that youngsters were fascinated by steam trains

Cheshire's finest is now to be found in Yorkshire: restreamlined after 62 years, Princess Coronation Pacific No 6229 Duchess of Hamilton *makes its debut at the National Railway Museum at York in May 2009 at the end of a four-year project to build a new streamlined casing. (Author)*

and what better than to be able to see the biggest and best close up, with a guide on hand to explain their history and finer details. *Duchess of Hamilton* was duly taken as a static exhibit to Butlins Minehead and *Duchess of Sutherland* to Butlins Heads of Ayr holiday camps. In 1976, the Friends of the National Railway Museum arranged for the York museum to take No 46229 on loan. Restored to running order, it returned to main line service in 1980, and in 1987 was bought by the museum.

Its ten-year boiler ticket ran out in 1998, and it became a static exhibit at York. However, in 2005, the museum announced a bold project to rebuild the streamlined casing, but to a slightly lower height than before, in case the opportunity arose for a full overhaul to main line condition. The work was undertaken at Tylseley Locomotive Works in Birmingham under the auspices of its chief engineer Bob Meanley, and on 18 May 2009 it was returned to the museum for display as a centrepiece of the Great Hall, reminding everyone of the days when Crewe turned out world beaters.

Duchess of Sutherland, which was built in July 1938 but never streamlined, was allocated to Crewe North depot on nationalisation. It was acquired from Butlins by Alan Bloom, founder of Bressingham Steam Museum in Norfolk. In turn, it was bought by the Princess Royal Class Locomotive Trust and restored to working order at the Midland Railway-Butterley.

Another proud moment for Crewe came on 11 June 2002, when No 6233 became the first steam locomotive for 35 years to haul the Royal Train, transporting Queen Elizabeth II from Holyhead to Llandudno Junction during a tour of North Wales as part of her Golden Jubilee. On 22 March 2005, the Duchess again hauled the Royal Train, taking Prince Charles from Settle to Carlisle. During the trip, the Prince spent 15 minutes behind the locomotive controls.

Two of the fabulous Britannia Pacifics also survive, in No 70000 *Britannia*, which was at one time owned by Pete Waterman and rebuilt at his LNWR works, and No 70013 *Oliver Cromwell*, part of the National Collection which was given a bolthole at Bressingham Steam Museum in Norfolk after the end of steam.

Thanks to the preservation movement, *Duchess of Sutherland*, *Duke of Gloucester*, both Britannias and several other classic locomotives can today be seen in action hauling special trains on the West Coast Main Line through Crewe and other main routes in Cheshire.

The restoration of No 71000 and its enhancement by volunteers saw the preservation sector learn many lessons. If a one-off partially dismembered locomotive can be rebuilt to be better than it was, surely it is possible, even without the benefit of a major railway workshop, to build a brand new main line steam locomotive from scratch?

Many new-build schemes big and small have been launched by the preservation movement, often with the aim of filling in gaps in the heritage era steam fleet left by the scrapping of the last remaining example of particular locomotive types. The best-known new-build project is A1 Pacific No 60163 *Tornado*, which took 18 years from conception to its main line debut in late January 2009, from when it has regularly made headlines.

One of the more recent new-build projects is to build – partially at Crewe – an example of the works' most successful 20th-century locomotives, in the form of a new three-cylinder LMS Patriot 4-6-0. It will not be a replica of the extinct class, but what would have been the next in line to be built, taking into account modifications to meet the requirements of today's national network. The Patriots were all withdrawn in 1960–62 and scrapped, the last being Nos 45543 and 45550.

Endorsed by the Royal British Legion, and built by the LMS-Patriot Project, it will remember those who gave their lives in two world wars and subsequent conflicts, and accordingly, will be numbered 45551 and named *The Unknown Warrior*.

The project was officially launched in April 2008 at the Llangollen Railway. In March 2009, the frame plates were cut by Corus Steel and, after machining, were taken to Llangollen where the locomotive is being assembled. A suitable tender from Barry scrapyard was received for the project, and following a £60,000 appeal by readers of *Heritage Railway* magazine to pay for the casting of six new driving wheels, the first was cast at Boro Foundry in Lye, West Midlands, on 13 September 2010.

LNWR Heritage Ltd has been chosen as the preferred builder of the boiler, the biggest and most expensive component. A target date of 2018 has been set for the completion of *The Unknown Warrior*, to coincide with the 100th anniversary of the signing of the Armistice which brought about an end to the First World War. The locomotive will become a steam version of the Cenotaph, taking on a role as the National Memorial Engine.

Another famous LNWR locomotive type which would have been very familiar to Cheshire passengers in mid-Victorian times is being recreated at Tyseley Locomotive Works.

In 1851, London & North Western Railway Southern Division locomotive superintendent James McConnell designed a series of powerful 2-2-2 express engines called 'Bloomers'. They took their nickname from women's liberation protagonist Amelia Bloomer, who wanted to reform contemporary female clothing to gain freedom of movement. When a handful of young women appeared in London in loose knee-length frocks and lightweight pants down to

Plans to build a new LMS Patriot, with the boiler being constructed at Crewe, are well advanced. The author stands in front of the first driving wheel to be cast, at Boro Foundry in Lye, West Midlands, in September 2010. (Author's Collection)

Showing too much wheel in an age when people referred to table supports rather than table legs: an LNWR Bloomer, named after Amelia Bloomer's outrageous fashions. (Illustrated London News)

the ankles, as she recommended, as opposed to tight-laced corsets with yards of flannel petticoats and crinolines, it sent out shock waves, but the fashion soon caught on. McConnell's new 2-2-2s also unashamedly showed all their wheels, and the nickname given by locomotive crews so quickly caught on that it was soon used in official correspondence, and the name firmly stuck.

The last Bloomer was withdrawn and scrapped in 1888, but a century later, Tyseley began building a new one with grant aid given to mark the 150th anniversary of the arrival of the railway in Birmingham. When complete, it will be numbered 670, the works' postal address in Warwick Road, Tyseley, following the LNWR practice of not having a numbering sequence for locomotives but often taking them from works numbers.

A project to build what would have been the next Clan Pacific, No 72010 *Hengist*, off the production line at Crewe, had the order for more Standard 6s not been cancelled by British Railways, was started by the Standard Steam Locomotive Company in 1995 and to date has produced many components including the frames. Next to Pete Waterman's works is Crewe Heritage Centre, a railway museum established in 1987 and located between the junction to the

Hardwicke, *the LNWR recordbreaker of the 1895 Races to the North, on display in the National Railway Museum at York.* (Author)

Chester line and West Coast Main Line, in a yard which was once part of Crewe Works. It has three signalboxes including the large, all-electric Crewe North Junction signalbox, which the public can operate and look around. It also has an extensive miniature railway with steam, diesel and electric traction, and standard gauge brake van rides are available on high days and holidays.

Its star outdoor exhibit is British Railway's pre-production 25kW overhead electric Class 370 Advance Passenger Train, at 8,000 hp the most powerful domestic train to have operated in Britain, which in December 1979 set a British rail speed record of 162.2 mph. Tom Clark might have been delighted, but the Class 370 never made it into production. Today it stands silent alongside the trunk line it was meant to serve, while *Princess Elizabeth* occasionally runs past.

It will take much more than modern transport technology to ever bring the final curtain down on the age of steam in Cheshire, a county which many travelled through rather than to, and yet which played a major role in world transport technology on steel wheels.

Index

Index